all the best

The best wine for pizza. The best wine to get the party started. The best wine for BBQ'd burgers. The best wine for chilling out. The best wine for steak. The best wine under ten dollars. The best wine for after work. The best wine for romance. The best local wine. The best wine to beat the heat. The best wine for the novice. The best wine for everyday meals. The best nice wine. The best wild wine. The best Shiraz. The best seducers.

The best wine book.

Written, produced and published by Billy Munnelly

Designed by Kato Wake
katowake@sympatico.ca

Printed by Commercial Printers in Stratford, Ontario
ISBN 0-9693717-5-6

Published every year since 1990

Additional copies available for $24.95
(tax and postage included) from

Billy's Best Bottles
589 Markham Street
Toronto Ontario
M6G 2L7

P 416 530 1545
F 415 530 1575
E info@billysbestbottles.com

www.billysbestbottles.com

Distributed to the retail trade by WHITECAP BOOKS,
Vancouver 604.980.9852

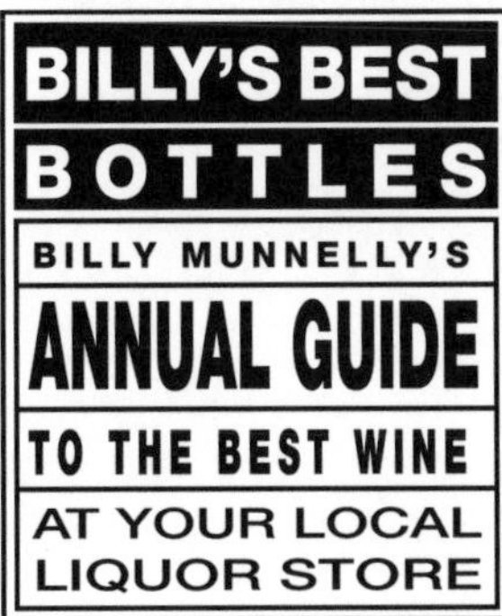

Not only ***the best wines*** *. . . but how* ***to use them***

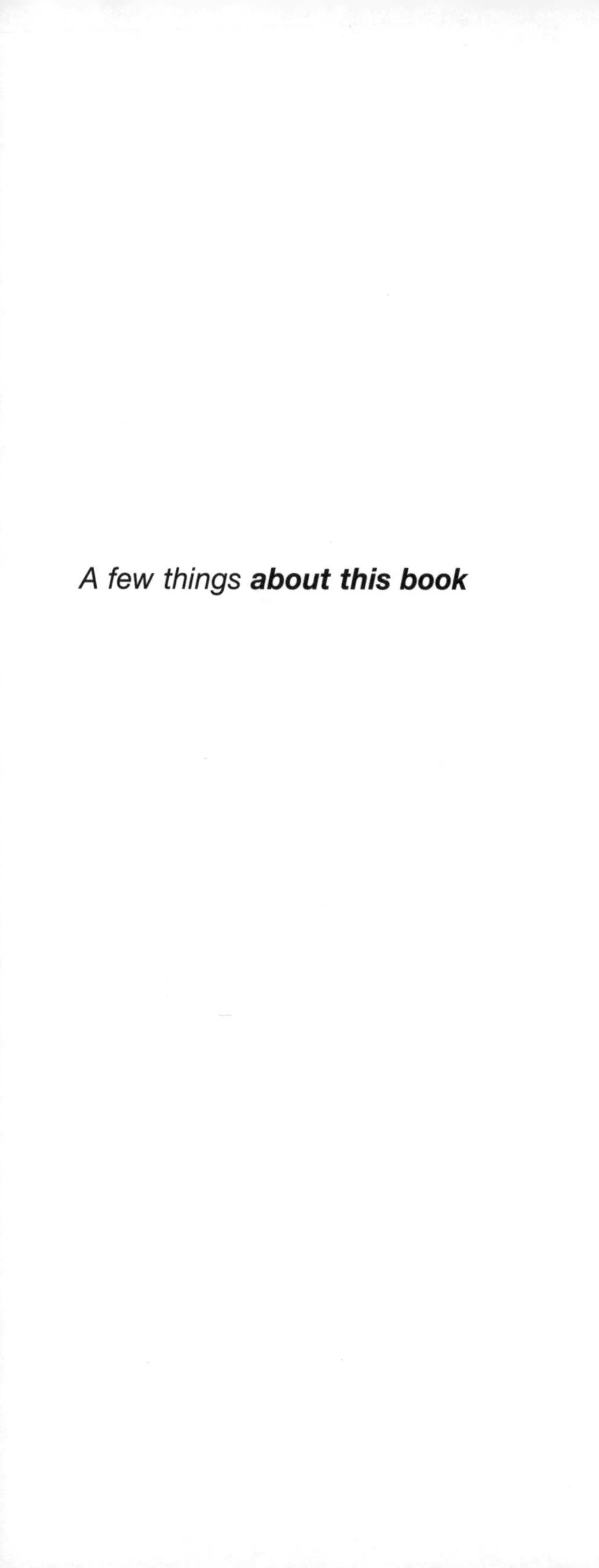

A few things ***about this book***

This book will help you

choose the best wine without spending a lot of time and money. This book is for people who enjoy variety in their drinking and are open to new experiences. This book is especially useful for the beginner, or for anyone who wants quick answers on which wine to buy. This book is about getting the most out of wines by drinking them in the context for which they are intended.

Each wine in this book is available at your local LCBO, or can be ordered. While most wine books celebrate the high and mighty of the wine world, my focus is on the middle ground, the good everyday, the trooper, the Toyota. Wines to get you through the week - and take you on the occasional trip. Wines to drink rather than worship.

I purchase and taste everything that the LCBO offers, and have published this book every year since 1990. Besides this handbook, I also publish Canada's largest circulation consumer wine guide, Billy's Best Bottles, which is celebrating its 21st year. Contact us if you would like a free trial issue.

MADE IN ONTARIO
BUT GOOD FOR ALL OTHER CANADIAN PROVINCES

While this book recommends the best wines offered in Ontario, many of them are available in other provinces. Simply supply the CSPC code number listed after the name of each wine and your store will be able to tell you if the wine is available or not.

my take on wine

I believe

My book is small because I do not believe you need to know all the facts about each wine – where it was produced, who made it, what type of grapes were used, etc. **My main interest is how a wine tastes and feels, and how it might fit into our lives.**

I drink the wines in this book not just because they are inexpensive, but because they give me the best times. Over the years I've noticed that we have the best relationships with places and pleasures that are not so big, important or grand. We like to be able to work fun into life and that happens more readily when we take the low road. The back street café over the fancy joint.

We live in a golden age of wine – the quality and value of low priced wine in particular has never been better. And the LCBO's stock is as diverse as what you'll find anywhere in the world. I think you'll agree once you start drinking your way through this book.

Before you ask "What's good?", you need to ask "What am I in the mood for?" **All the selections in my book are arranged by mood.**

I believe that a **wine book should offer updates** when vintages change. My web site will.

I believe that we have a great variety of wine styles because **our lives are filled with many different rhythms, moods and needs.** If we only had 'nice wine' we'd be in trouble, and bored.

For a wine buying book to be useful I think that it must offer **more than just a list of what to buy** – it must also advise on **when to drink the wines**.

If **you only buy Shiraz, you are missing out** on an awful lot of other wine pleasures. I often think that a good subtitle for this book might be "95 Wines To Drink When You're Tired of Shiraz."

Wine works according to a setting, a specific moment. **Great wine experiences do not require a great wine** – just one that's right for the context.

I believe that **a good wine is one that brings something desirable to the moment,** i.e. quenches your thirst, stimulates your palate, warms your belly, or takes you on a trip.

We are told that wine is about flavour – but it's not. The communion between people and wine is feeling. The essence or character of a wine can only be felt. It's the feeling that connects wine to our moods and events.

I think our pursuit of information, instead of understanding, has kept wine culture stuck in very traditional ways. We are still told that if we learn the names of all the great wines we will know what to buy, and thereby have a good time. It's all about being right, as opposed to what might please you. Prestige over pleasure. It's as silly as saying Mozart is great, play him and you'll be happy. What people need is not names but an understanding of the experience of the different wine styles – uplifting Dry Riesling, soothing Shiraz, challenging Sauvignon Blanc, etc.

I believe that **wine should be more than just a pleasant drink.** If you just want easy-drinking and smoothness, milk or pop is a far better buy. The purpose of wine is to be more interesting than these drinks – and that includes having features such as roughness, sharpness, extremes, complexity, and the unexpected. These are many of the same character aspects that make music, and life in general, stimulating. Emotion and tension are key in wine as they are in music. Sure, you'll find pleasant wine recommendations in this Handbook, but they are just part of the total lineup. If you want niceness exclusively, you do not need this guide.

For me, **wine and music play similar roles in life.** They both offer an endless variety of opportunities for a lift, a laugh, or to generally delight the heart and soul. For both wine and music, the key to enjoyment lies in developing a sense of what is appropriate – a knack for choosing the wine or music that's right for the moment. One minute we might desire something nourishing and soothing. Another time we want to kick up our heels and be wild. **Matching the spirit or character of a wine to that of an event is the great overlooked challenge in wine. The person who knows which wine 'to play' is the real wine expert.**

my system

I've always felt that part of the difficulty with wine has been that it's poorly defined. Stores and restaurants offer wine by country, price or grape variety, but this does not tell people what to expect. **Information about places, grapes, history and vintages do nothing to help us choose the right bottle to put on the table.** People can select the kind of music they want because the subject has well-defined categories – the person looking for opera never buys rock and roll by mistake.

The **WINE SPECTRUM chart** that you'll find on the next page is **my way of categorizing wine. It shows where wines fit in relation to each other, and it shows where they might fit into our lives.** All is explained in one chart. Everything you need in one formula.

Almost every decision made in life marks a spot on a spectrum of choices. Only by knowing what your choices are can you make a selection. My WINE SPECTRUM shows you what's available in the wine world, and tells you where you are once you choose. Where to go next is an easy decision because you know where you've been. Having a spectrum is like having a road map – something that helps you get where you want to be. Or helps you go elsewhere without getting lost.

The spectrum categories evolved through an understanding of our basic wine needs: something to drink with everyday meals (MEDIUM), something for richer times and foods (RICH), and something to refresh or to get an event started (FRESH or LIVELY). We need a total of six wines to cover these three needs because of the possibility of a red or white selection. **All wines chosen for this book are identified by their category – a 'when to drink it' guide. Take a minute to read the guide pages at the beginning of each category. Consider having a stock of all six categories on hand and you will be prepared for any mood or event.**

P.S. Sweet and fortified wines are in a section called 'FRINGE' which you'll find after the six main category picks.

How to use ***this book***

two wines – three times the fun

Buy two wines, a white from the Fresh section and a red from the Medium or Rich section. Enjoy a glass or two of the white, noting its liveliness. Recork and refrigerate it, and open the red. This drink will feel more nourishing. Having these two wine experiences is not just better, it satisfies our two basic needs – to be refreshed and to be nourished. Repeat this experience with different wines at different times. Branch out into the other categories. It's the only way to drink wine.

In this book you'll find the Fresh/Lively wines up front, the Rich ones towards the back, and the Mediums in the middle.

the 100 best wines

*and **when to drink** them*

fresh *white*

to refresh + stimulate
to quench your thirst

thirst-quenchers *to get things started*

- **Simple, fresh and maybe a little jolting.**
- **Assertive.**
- **Light and full of energy.**
- **Have before a meal, when you are thirsty or with 'fresh' appetizers. The equivalent of the lively music you'd play to get the party started.**
- **An opening act – not the main event. Always start with a FRESH wine to contrast with the wines that follow.**

food pairing: *antipasto, sushi, oysters, Asian foods, smoked salmon, goat cheese.*

watchpoint: *Don't overdo FRESH white wines. Their tartness can get annoying after a few glasses – like too much loud music. Refrigerated open bottles will keep well for 3 to 4 days.*

getting **started**

the first glass

***In the mood** for an opening act.*

Liveliness beats niceness if you want your event to get off the ground. That first glass should deliver a lift. A shot of energy. The best wine to get the evening or party started is Sparkling.

One of the delights in today's wine world is the availability of wonderful Sparkling wine at an everyday price. Make it one of your everyday drinks.

service

Serve well chilled in a simple narrow glass tumbler, or use a Champagne flute if you wish.

food ideas

All of these wines are good partners for appetizers or tapas-style foods. Good for cutting through salty appetizers (like tapenade), and elegant enough to pair with caviar and oysters.

I wouldn't dream of kicking off a party without **Prosecco Di Valdobbiadene 2002 Val d'Oca Brut, Italy** (#340570 $11.60). This Italian fizz is the most lighthearted sparkling wine in the world. It always produces a smile. Prosecco is drunk young because lightness and playfulness are its nature. The French have created an aura of luxury around Champagne, but the Italians believe that sparkling wine should be an everyday drink, at an everyday price.

Australia also believes in having fun with sparkling wine. **Jacob's Creek Brut Cuveé Chardonnay/Pinot Noir** (#562991 $13.25) is a fun wine that should be invited to every party.

Spain is the traditional home of bargain priced bubbly and **Codorniu Brut Classico, Spain** (#503490 $10.75) and **Segura Viudas Brut, Spain** (#158493 $11.45) are two of the best-tasting ten dollar wines in the world.

after **work** *refreshers*

*from our **local wineries***

***In the mood** for an after work refresher.*

Ontario Dry Riesling is one of the best refreshers in the world. It's our great contribution to the world of wine. A must try, especially when you're really thirsty – like in the summer months.

service

Glass tumblers or medium-sized glasses are best. The live wire nature of Dry Riesling is great for one or three glasses, but after that, you need to switch to a calmer, more nourishing wine.

food ideas

Raw oysters, smoked salmon and seafood appetizers are good food partners for Dry Riesling.

Cave Spring 2002 Dry Riesling, Niagara (#233635 $11.95). Cave Spring wrote the book on local Riesling with a style based on fresh, citrus flavours. The 2002 is certainly exhilarating and hair-raising.

Jackson-Triggs 2002 Dry Riesling 'Black Label', Niagara (#526277 $9.95) is crisp, but not tart, and the flavours have a nice hit of the tropics. Refreshing but also easy to sip.

Ch. des Charmes 2001 Riesling, Niagara (#61499 $9.95). Off-dry, but quite refreshing. You'll love the exotic and spicy flavours.

Henry of Pelham 2002 Dry Riesling, Niagara (#268375 $10.95) is terribly tart, invigorating and high-pitched. A fantastic summer thirst-quencher.

P.S. There are more local Rieslings in the Medium White section of this book.

F FRESH WHITE | L LIVELY RED | M MEDIUM WHITE | M MEDIUM RED | R RICH WHITE | R RICH RED

another after **work** *refresher*

Riesling again

In the mood *for a happy hour wine.*

Considering that most people want wines that are smooth, rich, heartwarming and sexy, I think we can safely say that Dry Riesling is the anti-wine. It's cold, lean, tart and quite the austere experience. Everything about it suggests the bare bones, monastic life. It's the puritan in the white wine world.

But pure can be good, even great. The pure air on a spring day or the pure nature of spring water are refreshing. Perrier is popular. A Mercedes does not offer the most luxurious ride but there is much to be said for the precision and refinement of the engineering. Purity of design and line can help us see things more clearly and refresh our vision.

Not everything in life needs to be nice and cuddly and this also applies to wine. There are moments when we want a refreshing jolt. We want a glass or two of Riesling.

service

Glass tumblers or medium-sized glasses are best. The live wire nature of Dry Riesling is great for one or three glasses, but after that you need to switch to a calmer, more nourishing wine.

food ideas

Raw oysters, smoked salmon and seafood appetizers are good food partners for Dry Riesling.

Riesling is hugely popular in Australia, where all the bottles are now screw topped. Try **Wolf Blass 2003 Riesling, South Australia** (#505370 $11.95) for after work or weekend sipping.

Peter Lehmann 2001 Riesling, Barossa, Australia (#636993 $12.95) is more challenging – classic, austere Riesling. Not for everyone, but if you're looking for a dry, martini-style wine, this will certainly deliver the lift.

New Zealand's **Stoneleigh 2003 Riesling** (#527713 $11.95) has Granny Smith apple crunch and purity. Lime flavours add to the tingle. Quite similar to our local Rieslings.

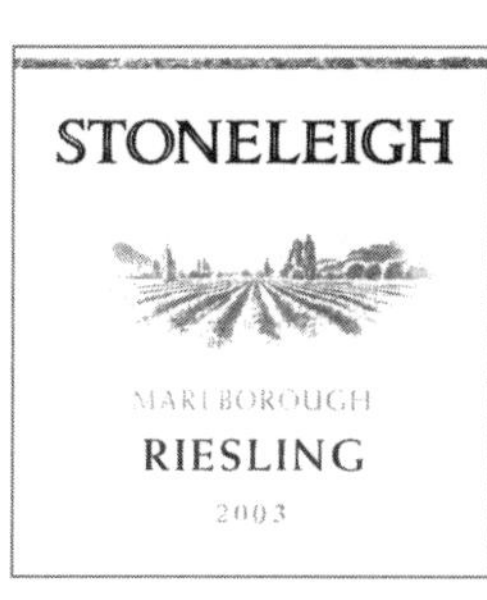

real live **wires**

wines for a lift

In the mood *for a refresher.*

The exuberant, fresh statement of Sauvignon Blanc is often likened to a spring breeze, but in some cases it's more like a winter gale. It's the 'wild thing' of wine – wine with attitude. It's the jolt we desire when our mood is to feel more alive, to have a lift. The palate is certainly keener after a glass of Sauvignon.

Sauvignon Blanc is today's most exciting white wine category because it's so distinctive, and because the overall quality is very high. Like Chardonnay, it comes in different styles. Here we meet the aperitif/ refresher edition.

service

Sauvignon needs to be served really cold. A medium-sized glass is good, but for casual times a tumbler or juice glass will fit the offbeat nature of the wine.

food ideas

Goat cheese, asparagus, sushi, oysters, chicken with herbs, shrimp and most appetizers.

Stoneleigh 2003 Sauvignon Blanc, Marlborough, New Zealand (#293043 $14.05) has a bracing spring breeze feeling. Wonderfully refreshing in the mouth. A great ambassador for New Zealand Sauvignon.

Mad Fish 2003 Semillon/Sauvignon Blanc, Western Australia (#588863 $14.95) is pure energy. Wonderful citrusy flavours along with the cool feeling of the ocean.

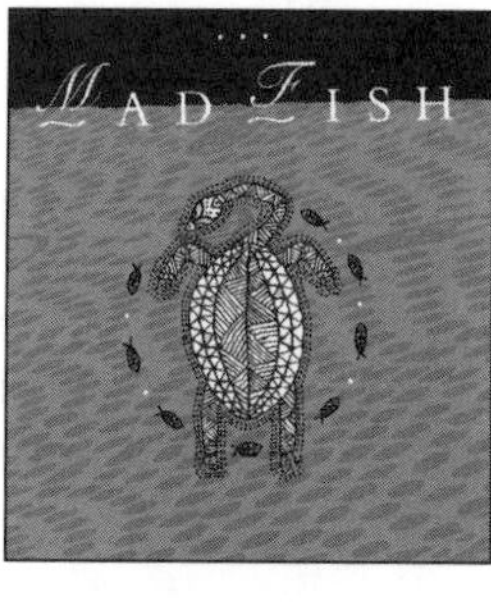

Wolf Blass 2003 Sauvignon Blanc, Australia (#611475 $14.95) offers good, frank refreshment with lemony zest. Low alcohol invites gulping.

P.S. There are more Sauvignon Blancs in the Medium White section of this book.

dry
but not too
yummy and refreshing

In the mood *for a white wine that is slightly sweet but still refreshingly dry.*

Honest – it is possible to find a white wine with sweet fruit flavours that is also refreshingly dry. Wines made from Gewurztraminer, Muscat or Riesling grapes often have this quality. They are called the aromatic family of wines. Try my selections and you'll see what I mean. I've seen many a non-drinker lose their self-control after a sip or two of Gewurztraminer.

The hit of flavour in aromatic wines sedates the palate so we tend not to gulp them as quickly as we might bone-dry wines. Something to keep in mind if your drinking starts long before your eating.

service
Serve well chilled. You could echo the fun of these wines by serving them in odd-shaped glasses.

food ideas
Shrimp, spring rolls, mild curries, egg dishes, salads and alfresco lunches, of course.

Chateau Bonnet 2002 Bordeaux, France (#83709 $12.95) is one of the world's great, fun whites. A must for parties or Sunday brunch. Works equally well for both the novice and the seasoned wino.

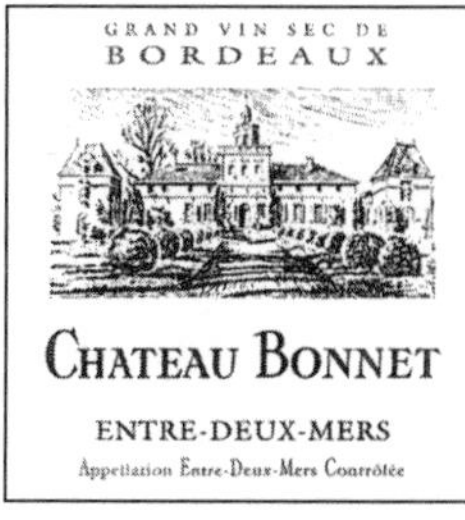

Inniskillin 2002 Riesling, Niagara (#83790 $10.45). The expression here is of lightness and good cheer. A 'be happy' wine. Shades of a spritzer with a squeeze of lemon.

Jackson-Triggs 2002 Gewurztraminer 'Black Label', Niagara (#526269 $9.95) is super refreshing. The Gewurz spice is just a tease . . . fun, fun stuff. One of the best 'anytime' drinks in the store. Don't be without an open bottle.

beat *the* heat

wines to sip on the dock

***In the mood** for quenching your thirst on a hot summer day.*

Summer days are better with Vinho Verde. That may sound like a commercial, but it's the truth. Vinho Verde is a peasant wine from the north of Portugal that is slightly spritzy, keenly tart and as pure as spring water. You can guzzle it freely because it has 50% less alcohol than the average Chardonnay. Austrian wines also have the keen edge that's necessary to handle summer thirst. Aligoté is a French thirst-quencher and Chateau des Charmes makes a good version of it in Niagara.

service

Serve these wines icy cold in tumbler glasses. No need for stemware.

food ideas

Whatever is around for snacks. These wines are mainly about gulping, not pairing with food.

Sogrape N/V Vinho Verde 'Gazela', Portugal (#141432 $7.90). Seriously dry, spritzy and a lot like biting into a Granny Smith apple. Refreshment – with a jolt. Flavour is not part of the scene. Such is the nature of Vinho Verde.

Winzer Krems 2001 Riesling/Müller Thurgau, Austria (#573329 $8.95). Truly invigorating – with the sharp edge that's the hallmark of Austrian white wine. And there's just enough flavour to keep your taste buds entertained.

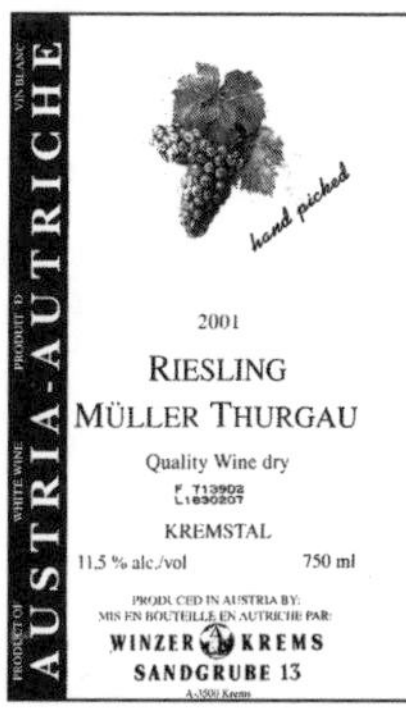

Ch. des Charmes 2002 Aligoté, Niagara (#284950 $10.95) is crisp and clean, which is how it's suppose to be. Frank refreshment for a hot day. Good luncheon wine too.

▪ the in-fashion *refresher*

Pinot Grigio

In the mood *for a good, everyday, refreshing white wine.*

Pinot Grigio is the new trendy wine. It's the equivalent of easy listening music – something to have when Chardonnay or Sauvignon might be too much. It has a nice, easy-to-like character – not very flavourful, but friendly.

the gist: *Pinot Grigio is a light, simple, anytime quaff. A little something for life's quieter moments and meals. It's ideal for lazy summer events.*

in Italy: *The style of Pinot Grigio varies from region to region – the difference being in the degree of dryness. Veneto wines are gentle and agreeable, while Friuli produces pure, classy wines for seafood. In Trentino, Grigio is tart and super refreshing.*

a good thing: *Italy puts Pinot Grigio (and most of its other whites) in clear glass bottles. I feel this delivers the message of the wine's style – a refresher, to be drunk young.*

service

Serve well chilled in a tumbler or medium-sized glass.

food ideas

Everyday meals that call out for a simple white wine.

Mezza Corona 2002 Pinot Grigio, Trentino, Italy (#302380 $11.95) tingles in the mouth with a lovely mix of mineral, floral and lemon flavours. Refreshment and fun. Lovely, lovely stuff.

Lamberti 2002 Pinot Grigio 'Santepietre', Veneto, Italy (#560524 $10.35). Gentle on my mind wine that may remind you of your first kiss – sweet and innocent. Wine to chill out with . . . stop the world and unwind. No food, no loud music.

Collavini 2002 Pinot Grigio, Friuli, Italy (#33340 $13.95). Classic Italian white wine – crisp and pure with just a little flavour. Like the perfect party guest – it's well turned out and cheerful.

P.S. There are more Pinot Grigios reviewed in the Medium White section of this book.

to start
a special occasion
the classy cocktail

In the mood *for starting with something special.*

It is not well known, but most Champagnes belong to the fresh category of wines. Champagnes labeled Brut are particularly invigorating. Sip at the cocktail hour. Champagne's glamourous aura shines brightest as the opening act – before a nice meal.

service
Serve Champagne cold and use a stemmed or 'fluted' glass. Open carefully, keeping the bottle angled at 45° and pointing it away from valued friends and possessions! Pour slowly so the foam has time to settle.

food ideas
Sip at the cocktail hour without food. Slivers of parmesan cheese, however, are a good mate with Champagne.

Pol Roger Brut Champagne (#51953 $45.95) is austere but deliciously teasing – the classic aperitif.

Nicolas Feuillatte Brut Champagne, France (#537605 $41.95) is equally good at this job – a real live wire. Bold, tart and uplifting.

Piper Heidsieck Brut Champagne, France (#361626 $43.00) is high-spirited with a lighthearted feeling. Certainly of the cocktail spirit.

lively red

to celebrate the everyday refreshing reds

for lighter everyday meals

- **These wines feel fresher and livelier than all other reds. Lightly chilled, they offer some of the refreshing qualities of whites.**
- **Enjoy when the mood (and food) is light-hearted – lunch, early evening, pizza night and summer picnics.**
- **Part of your house wine stock.**
- **Social wines that give everyday pleasure and aid digestion. The refreshing nature of these wines is more welcome at parties than the heavier, richer reds.**
- **Always serve lightly chilled.**

food pairing: *roast chicken, pizza and burgers, tomato pasta, grilled chicken, snacks, tapas, sandwiches, Indian curry*

watchpoint: *Drink and enjoy all LIVELY REDS without too much fuss. It is essential to lightly chill these wines. Refrigerated open bottles will keep well for 3 to 4 days.*

& merlot cabernet
the lighter side
Italian style

***In the mood** for a lighthearted, every-day red – at a lighthearted price.*

The rich and expensive variety of Merlot and Cabernet is the most well known, but some regions produce a lighter style wine that's fun to drink with everyday meals. These wines will appeal most to those who enjoy the very dry, traditional European wines – they may not work for the Shiraz fan.

service

Serve slightly chilled in simple glasses. Five minutes in the freezer before serving works!

food ideas

Simple everyday meals – pizza or burgers. These wines are perfect partners for tomato sauced pasta dishes too. These wines NEED food – not for sipping.

Cesari 2002 Merlot Delle Venezie, Italy (#572453 $6.50) has delicious, plummy/sweet flavours, a bright 'n cheerful personality and a refreshing tang. Hard to beat for house wine. Chill a notch.

Lamberti 2001 Merlot/Sangiovese, Veneto, Italy (#517623 $9.85) is so lively it almost climbs out of the glass to meet you. It's brisk, it's keen, it's invigorating – imagine a ride on a Vespa. Don't forget to stop for bruschetta or pizza.

Local Cabernet Franc is lighthearted, herbaceous and a good brisk drink for everyday foods. **Inniskillin 2002 Cabernet Franc, Niagara** (#317016 $11.95) is a playful wine with bright fruit flavours and tremendous vitality. Wine for a lift.

Colio 'Harrow Estates' 2002 Cabernet Franc, Ontario (#297184 $9.95) has a nice, friendly, everyday quality. And is great with food. Ideal house or party wine.

Ancient Coast 2002 Cabernet Franc, Niagara (#559195 $9.95) is certainly lively and tart. Delicious berry flavours.

best partners for pizza + pasta

Italian exuberance

***In the mood** for lively red wine to partner with the above.*

You would never have to ask for a lively red in an Italian café. It's usually the only kind they serve. Italian food is exuberant and so are Italian wines. They refresh and they encourage lighthearted, fun times. The lesson to learn from Italy is to keep wine simple but enjoy it often. At least once a day.

service

Serve slightly chilled in simple glasses. Five minutes in the freezer before serving works!

food ideas

Simple everyday meals – pizza or burgers. These wines are perfect partners for tomato sauced pasta dishes too. These wines NEED food – not for sipping.

Bersano 2001 Barbera 'Costalunga' Piedmont, Italy (#348680 $11.95) is red wine with the sock-it-to-you character of tomato sauce. Very good, very Italian. Challenging, but great when you're in the mood for it. Super refreshing and appetizing. Born to be with pizza or pasta.

Rocco Delle Macie 2002 Chianti 'Vernaiolo', Italy (#269589 $9.95) is a spirited, dynamic, young Chianti at a decent price. Packed with gusto, it's mighty refreshing and tangy enough to get you through the biggest pizza, bowl of pasta or platter of bruschetta.

It would be hard to find a better example of spirited Italian red wine than **Citra 2002 Montepulciano D'Abbruzzo, Italy** (#446633 $6.65). So tasty and so generous. Great with hearty pasta, spicy sausages or even a steak. May be the best red wine value in the world.

Spinelli 2001 Montepulciano D'Abruzzo 'Quartana', Italy (#454629 $6.45) feels like it never left Italy. The spirited, earthy character will make your pizza taste 'more' Italian.

really refreshing

the beaujolais style

fun, drink-me-quick reds

In the mood *for red wine for lively times – everyday meals, picnics in the park or parties.*

How can red wine be refreshing? The production technique for some reds, such as Beaujolais, results in wine with the characteristics of a white. No tannins. So they are intended to be chilled (lightly) and gulped. I'll tell ya, once you've had a few cool glasses of a fresh red you may never go back to white wines. The perfect 'starter red' for your friends who swear they don't like red wine.

Summer is the season for these wines because they compliment almost all foods of that season and bring cheer to any event. But I include chilled, fresh reds at parties all year round because of their light-hearted nature.

service

Serve slightly chilled in simple glasses. Five minutes in the freezer before serving works!

food ideas

Summer foods and salads. Roast chicken. No-brainer food.

Mommessin 2002 Beaujolais-Villages, France (#538959 $13.90) and **Georges Duboeuf 2002 Beaujolais-Villages, France** (#122077 $12.90) are wines with an equal hit of fruitiness and tartness. Wines that delight and energize. Exactly what you need in your glass on a hot summer afternoon or at a lively party. Lightly chill.

Thorin 2002 Côtes du Ventoux 'Grand Reserve Des Challieres', France (#331090 $8.90) is made by the same process as Beaujolais. Bright, juicy flavours are nicely edged with a refreshing bite. There's a shine and a vitality that says 'enjoy'. I bet you will. Everyday red wines don't get much better.

Lamberti 2002 Valpolicella 'Santepietre', Italy (#560508 $10.45) could hardly be more lively. A fruity, bright, refreshing wine that feels youthful and joyful. The true spirit of Valpolicella. A wine that deserves to be a lot better known.

real men drink **dry rosé**

think pink *for summer + fun*

In the mood *for wines for outdoor summer meals, picnics or parties.*

North Americans don't take Rosé seriously because it is associated with Blush – the 'soda pop' wine. Travel to Spain or the south of France, however, and we discover a different kind of Rosé – one with serious credentials – being enjoyed on a daily basis. Even the men drink it.

> ***P.S.*** *In the summer, the LCBO puts out a great array of Rosé from all parts of the world.* ***Vin Gris de Cigare*** *from* ***Bonny Doon*** *(California) is usually one of my favourites.*

service

Buy a selection and have a few bottles open. Rosé looks more attractive in a group, brightening the tabletop in the same way that flowers do. Chill as you would with whites, but if you're having Rosé with meals, leave the bottle out of the ice. It will develop more flavours as it warms up.

food ideas

Any food that you'd want to eat outdoors would be the right partner for Rosé: antipasto dishes, appetizers, salads of all kinds and fish or seafood. Salmon with Rosé is not only a match of pretty colours but also of spirits. While Rosé wines may give the impression of being lighthearted, many are deliberately high in alcohol in order to handle the oil and garlic of Mediterranean foods such as paella or couscous. And don't be afraid of a little hot spice. Rosé has Latin blood.

P.S. Rosé is mainly a summertime, outdoors drink but it's a great partner for turkey so keep it in mind for Christmas and Thanksgiving too.

Torres 2002 Rosado 'De Casta', Spain (#619916 $9.95) has the richness to partner with food, but it's also quite refreshing. It is classic Mediterranean Rosé with spicy fruit flavours.

JeanJean 2002 Rosé Syrah 'Arabesque' VDP d'Oc, France (#355347 $8.95) combines the refreshment of dry white wine with the savoury flavour of Syrah. Close to Provençe-style but a lot less expensive. Good house Rosé. Attractive package too.

Lamberti 2002 Bardolino Chiaretto 'Santepietre', Veneto, Italy (#396572 $8.90) is lightbodied and lighthearted Rosé with a refreshing spritz. There's a delicate fruitiness. Could not be better for lazy time sipping. Best for any outdoor times.

Xanadu 2002 Rosé of Cabernet, Western Australia (#587790 $11.50). Don't let the pale colour fool you. This is big wine in the Provençe style. For seafood or any well seasoned meat or vegetable dish. Have a refresher first, then indulge.

refreshing + *charming*

playful Pinot

In the mood *for a red that's yummy and lighthearted.*

Lighthearted and charming is a combination that you might not be familiar with but it's part of the appeal of Pinot Noir wine. I'm sure you'll become a fan once you taste the wine on the next page. Pinot Noir is a great seducer.

service

Serve lightly chilled and drink from a medium-sized glass.

food ideas

Burgers, chicken, grilled salmon or mushroom risotto.

Mission Hill 2001 Pinot Noir 'Bin 99' Okanagan Valley, British Columbia
(#118844 $12.95).
Purists get upset when I recommend this wine because it's a bit of a doll, a tart. So be warned – you might be seduced by a wine with no brains. But you could have a lot of fun, especially if you cook something spicy (with cumin or coriander) and light a candle or two. Mission Hill's Pinot is big on romance – I think of it as a west coast hippy that lived in Morocco. Lightly chill so you don't overheat.

P.S. This makes a great party drink too.

medium
white

wines in the mid-range
to celebrate everyday

for everyday meals

not light, not rich – just medium!

- **Affordable house wines.**
- **Social wines that give everyday pleasure and aid in digestion.**
- **Some days they will feel heavenly, at other times just good company.**

food pairing: *chicken or pork, fish, cream sauced pasta dishes, fish, seafood and egg dishes.*

watchpoint: *Drink and enjoy all MEDIUM white wines without too much fuss. Refrigerated open bottles will keep well for 3 to 4 days.*

good for *everyday* **meals +** **parties**

from our ***local wineries***

In the mood *for the above.*

Chardonnay has become synonymous with fullness and richness but this is not always so. Some Chardonnays are more everyday, more moderate – just right for weeknight supper or for weekend fun. House wine.

Local winemakers have good reason to be proud of what they have achieved in this category. These wines are on par with similarly priced imports.

service

Have your first glass well chilled and refreshing, but then let the wine warm up a bit to bring out the flavours. Use medium-sized glasses.

food ideas

Chicken, pork, seafood or pasta in a cream sauce.

Henry of Pelham 2002 Chardonnay 'Non Oaked', Niagara (#291211 $11.95) is fun because it starts out tart and refreshing – but on the second glass it gives you the sweetish kisses that tell you it's Chardonnay.

Jackson-Triggs 2002 Chardonnay 'Black Label', Niagara (#526251 $10.45) is bold, flavourful and tangy. Everyday Chardonnay for grilled foods. Niagara's answer to the big selling Aussie brands.

Pelee Island 2002 Chardonnay 'Premium Select', Ontario (#216044 $10.95) has lots of vitality and is less 'cute' than many Chardonnays. The country lad of local Chardonnays.

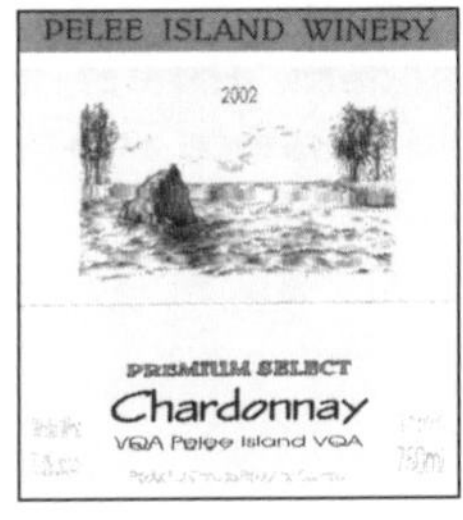

Colio 'Harrow Estates' 2002 Chardonnay, Ontario (#432062 $8.95) is tasty and cheerful. Enjoy any-time. Excellent party sipper or partner for light foods.

good for everyday meals + parties

*the **imports***

***In the mood** for the above.*

France has always been well known for expensive wines but recently it has also become quite good at producing quality, everyday-priced wines. The packaging still looks traditional but the wines are thoroughly modern. Expect a combination of old-world elegance and new-world friendliness.

service

Have your first glass well chilled and refreshing, but then let the wine warm up a bit to bring out the flavours. Use medium-sized glasses.

food ideas

Chicken, pork, seafood or pasta in a cream sauce.

Rothschild 2002 Chardonnay VDP d'Oc, France (#497528 $9.95) is keenly tart and refreshing. Good stuff for house wine.

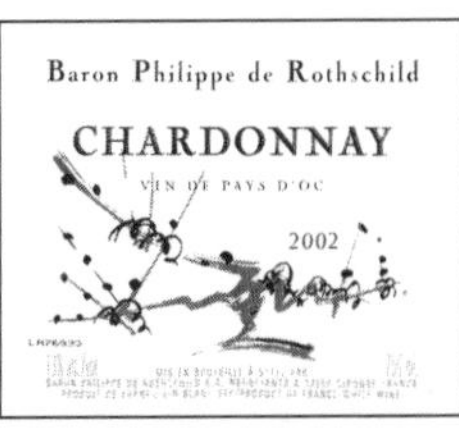

Fortant de France 2002 Chardonnay, VDP d'Oc, France (#256560 $8.95) is full and flavourful. Very Chardonnay-*ish.*

Georges Duboeuf 2001 Côtes du Rhône, France (#162404 $10.25) has the bright, joyful feeling of the yellow sunflowers shown on the label of the bottle. How clever.

Georges Duboeuf 2002 Macon-Villages, France (#110122 $12.45). Hits some of the glamour notes that make Chardonnay so popular. Lovely to sip after work, or at a party.

Bouchard Père & Fils 2002 Macon Lugny St. Pierre, France (#51573 $12.95). A delicious, delicate version of Chardonnay. Good for lazy times and a lovely wine to sip with friends who are not big wine fans.

JeanJean 2002 Chardonnay 'Arabesque' VDP d'Oc, France (#630681 $8.95) is pleasant and bargain priced. The sexy curved bottle is a bonus.

wines *for the* ***birds***

Serving fowl – ***serve Semillon***

In the mood *for a roast chicken dinner or the Christmas or Thanksgiving turkey.*

There is a new style of wine out there and I think you're going to enjoy it. No, it will not seduce you like Chardonnay, not thrill you like Sauvignon – this is 'sauce' wine. Wines made from the Semillon grape have a distinctive savoury quality that puts them right at the top of 'the best for food' category. Think sage-and-onion stuffing. Think of wine for the big bird, or the pleasure of a simply roasted or grilled chicken that's been rubbed with fresh herbs.

service

Serve chilled in a decent sized wine glass. Or a tumbler for summer lunch.

food ideas

Thanksgiving, Christmas and all the trimmings. Roasted or grilled chicken.

Calvet Reserve 2002 Bordeaux, France (#144568 $10.95) is Semillon with some Sauvignon. Austere, racy, invigorating and exciting. And challenging. The savoury flavours are fantastic with chicken.

Peter Lehmann 2001 Semillon, Barossa, Australia (#572412 $12.95) offers the savoury flavours of the grape and a mellow sweetness. Very appetizing, very yummy.

Tyrrell's 2002 Long Flat White, Australia (#183715 $9.90) has the Semillon character along with a pleasant, everyday drink quality. Once you get hooked on Semillon you'll be making this your house white. Great value.

Mission Hill 2002 Sauvignon Blanc, Okanagan Valley, British Columbia (#118893 $11.95) has a personality crisis – it wants to be a Semillon. And it should be, because it's a good one.

Xanadu 'Secession' 2001 Semillon/ Chardonnay, Western Australia (#599188 $14.35) is part savoury, part exotic. Has the high-spirited, invigorating character of Western Australian whites. Great with food and fun to sip too. Stylish package.

a walk on the **wild side**

Sauvignon Blanc – rarin' to go

***In the mood** to kick-start your taste buds.*

Sauvignon Blanc is the modern one in the world of white wine. It is high spirited and fun to drink. Although flavourful, it feels light. Chardonnay may be sexy, but Sauvignon is cool. And cool is better than sexy!

Sauvignon is catching our attention for the same reasons that Asian food did – bright flavours and new sensations for the mouth. Wineries are taking a fresh look at Sauvignon, as they see customer interest in lighter, leaner, jazzier wine – something to turn to after the Chardonnay era.

service

Sauvignon needs to be really cold. A medium-sized glass is good, but for casual times a small tumbler or juice glass will fit the offbeat nature of the wine.

food ideas

Seafood, Thai dishes, mildy spicy/hot foods. Any food that welcomes a 'squirt of lime' or a 'sprig of coriander' is a good partner for this wine. Cuisines in which the elements don't melt together, but bounce off each other, are also natural partners for Sauvignon.

Nederburg 2002 Sauvignon Blanc, South Africa (#382713 $9.95) is a high energy, razor edged wine. Great for seafood, or as an aperitif.

Santa Rita 2003 Sauvignon Blanc Reserva, Chile (#275677 $11.95) is another fab performance from this winery. Flavourful, zesty, jazzy, sexy Sauvignon doing the tango. A very exciting drink.

Serego Alighieri 2002 Bianco, Veneto, Italy (#409862 $12.95) does the live wire thing but there is also a sensational flavour show. A great drink. Most improved wine of the year.

Villa Maria 2002 Sauvignon Blanc, Marlborough, New Zealand (#426601 $13.95) is a WOW experience for sure. Supercharged, gale force white wine to get you going. The herbaceous/grassy experience of New Zealand's best.

Ch. Grand Renom 2001 Sauvignon, Bordeaux, France (#619859 $11.25) has the live wire Sauvignon character and the distinctive herbaceous/citrus flavours – but there is also a traditional wine sense. A great food wine.

Dry Riesling

classy *whites*

the freshly starched shirt

In the mood *for elegance. While these Dry Rieslings work well with almost any seafood or white meat, the main reason to select them is for their elegant, formal feeling.*

Riesling is confusing because it is made in many different styles. Earlier in the book I recommended a few live wire varieties for refreshment – here you'll find wines with a little more flesh on them. Wines with the cool and elegant feeling of starched white cotton.

service

Served well chilled in fine glassware. If you pour Dry Riesling before dinner and finish the bottle with seafood appetizers, your dinner party will be off to a great start. Your friends will think you are a wine wizard. In the summer, give these wines a table in the sun with a white tablecloth and a vase of flow ers. Think bright Matisse colours.

food ideas

Shrimp/seafood appetizers – needs a formal dinner party event.

Cave Spring 2002 Riesling Reserve, Niagara (#286377 $15.95) and **Henry of Pelham 2002 Riesling Reserve, Niagara** (#28391 $12.65) have mineral flavours that seem to vibrate in the glass. Wines to set you up – to tease or to echo the fresh feeling in seafood. Great vitality.

Hillebrand 2002 Riesling 'Trius', Niagara (#303792 $14.95) is fruitier and less formal than the above two wines. Lovely stuff. Delicious to sip.

P.S. There are more Dry Rieslings in the Fresh White section of this book.

kicking up the flavour

everyday whites with bold flavours

In the mood *for a bit of a show.*

Some moods or foods call for the bold flavoured wines we associate with sunny Australia or California. BBQ time for sure. But can we do it without getting into something too rich or expensive? Of course. All of the wines opposite cost less than ten dollars. They are perfect partners for the world of buttery/sweet and charred foods.

service

Serve chilled in a decent sized glass so the flavour can come out to meet you.

food ideas

Anything from the BBQ – especially chicken, salmon or shrimp, with lots of herbs and spices.

Hardys 2002 Chardonnay/Semillon 'Stamp Series', Australia (#335638 $8.95). It's all here – a blast of tropical fruit flavours, zesty vitality and a lemony tang. Yummy. Generous but not over the top, and a keen edge to keep us refreshed. Perfect!

Dom. Paul Mas 'La Forge' 2002 Chardonnay, VDP d'Oc, France (#580158 $8.95) is bold and tangy with Aussie-style richness and tropical flavour. Amazing amount of character for the price.

Bodegas Etchart 2002 Torrontés, Argentina (#283754 $9.95) combines exotic Muscat flavours with richness. Shades of a south seas island Chardonnay. Lots of perfume and show. But it is also refreshing. A novel house wine, aperitif or partner for herbed/spicy chicken. P.S. Torrontés is a native Argentinian grape that is a dead ringer for Muscat.

grigio *again*

Pinot Grigio for everyday meals

In the mood *for good, everyday wine that does not have the name Chardonnay on the label.*

We got introduced to some playful Pinot Grigios earlier in the Fresh section of this book – now it's time to meet some more of the family. These are a bit fuller and fleshier – wines for comfort foods.

service

Serve chilled. Pinot Grigio is more fun and family-style than formal, so use glassware that's in keeping with the wine style.

food ideas

Home cooking! Herbed roasted chicken and mashed potatoes. Or a wedge of quiche.

Vallagarina 2002 Pinot Grigio 'Nuvole', Trentino, Italy (#637611 $8.95). Crafted for complexity as well as refreshment. Very attractive fruity and spicy flavours. Fun to sip anytime – a wonderful drink.

Santi 2002 Pinot Grigio 'Sortesele', Trentino, Italy (#637603 $11.95) is super fresh and fruity. A refresher, an aperitif, a wine for seafood, a wine for lunch – a wine for a lift, a wine for parties. All the stuff that Pinot Grigio does well.

Talus 2002 Pinot Grigio, California (#611863 $10.95). Just a tease of flavour – no flashy Californian stuff. Honest, good everyday wine. Very Italian*esque*, right down to the arty label. Partner with its mate, Talus Shiraz, and your evening will be perfect.

Yes!
Pinot Gris and Pinot Grigio are the same thing.

a trio of **bargains**

cheap but good

In the mood *for budget wines.*

Don't ask me how they do it, but there are always a few people who deliver the goods for less.

service

Chill and enjoy. To chill a wine quickly a) throw it in the freezer for 10 minutes or b) put it in a bucket or sink filled with ice AND water for about 10 minutes. Adding salt to the water will melt the ice and chill your wine quicker.

food ideas

Everyday meals that call out for a simple white wine.

Marques de Riscal 2002 Rueda, Spain (#36822 $7.85) is not just a cheap date, it's a delicious wine. Fresh, fruity and fun. I've been a fan for years but this is the best vintage yet.

Dunavar 2002 Pinot Blanc, Hungary (#565820 $6.95) has the likeable, mild-mannered nature of this grape and a good hit of freshness – what more does one need in a budget-priced wine? Best as an after work pick-me-up, party wine or partner for light foods.

Dom. Boyar 2002 Chardonnay, Bulgaria (#428540 $6.95) is made in the pretty, slightly sweet, crowd-pleasing style. Good partner for spicy foods. And a lovely party drink.

medium *red*

wines in the mid-range to celebrate the everyday

*for **everyday celebrations** and hearty meals*

- **House wines which have a fullness, but stop short of being rich.**
- **Social wines that give everyday pleasure and aid in digestion.**
- **Some are good for everyday foods, while others have the character for dinner parties.**

food pairing: *mainly dark meats – ribs, burgers, casseroles, BBQs, sausages.*

watchpoint: *Best enjoyed from a large wineglass. Refrigerated open bottles will keep well for 3 to 4 days.*

best for **burgers**

check this out

In the mood *for wine to wash down your best burger.*

There are probably as many ideas of what constitutes a good burger as there are people who enjoy them. The best wine choice is sure to be subjective too. Here's mine. Because burgers offer instant gratification, I select a wine that tastes good from the first sip. The wine must also have an appetizing bite because I want the last mouthful of food to taste as good as the first. New World, fruity wines are usually best, especially if you like to load up on burger fixings. As ever, it's a mood thing. But not a matter of life and death.

service

Serve in tumblers or medium-sized glasses.

food ideas

Burgers or meatloaf.

Henry of Pelham 2002 Baco Noir, Niagara (#270926 $11.95) will appeal to those who enjoy reds with an exuberant vitality. It's Ontario's most distinctive red – a little quirky. A light chill brings out the magic. With a burger it tastes like a million bucks.

Rosemount 2002 Shiraz/Cabernet, Australia (#214270 $12.95) must surely have been created by the burger gods. Or by someone who's spent many an evening tuning in to the flavours and feelings created by a BBQ'd burger. It makes the experience bigger and richer – and does it with a sense of play. Lightly chill.

Torres 2001 Sangre de Toro, Spain (#6285 $10.95) has the out-to-please nature of a burger. Spicy and nourishing.

Sogrape Douro 2000 'Vila Regia', Portugal (#464388 $7.70) is a rustic red with a nourishing warmth and gutsy character. I like the frank everyday quality and everyday price.

F FRESH WHITE
L LIVELY RED
M MEDIUM WHITE
M MEDIUM RED
R RICH WHITE
R RICH RED

best for **value**

cheap but ***good***

In the mood *for quality, inexpensive wines.*

The old wine countries of Europe still find a way to produce really good wines for seven, eight and nine dollars. Cheers to that!

service

Serve in tumblers or medium-sized glasses. Lightly chill.

food ideas

Everyday food.

Cantina Tollo 2000 Montepulciano D'Abruzzo 'Colle Secco', Italy (#195826 $8.25) may seem tart at first but it doesn't take long to reveal its warm heart. Woodsy, Chianti-style wine. Lots of character for the price.

Aveleda 2000 Douro 'Charamba', Portugal (#352963 $8.10) is a really vibrant café wine that may remind you of Chianti. Spirited and nourishing. Most improved red wine in the store.

Sogrape 2000 Douro 'Mateus Signature', Portugal (#308643 $7.95) is a lightish, everyday red with appetizing plummy flavours. Tasty and tangy. A consistent performer.

Umani Ronchi 2001 Rosso Conero 'Serrano', Italy (#521096 $9.95) is a beefier, richer edition of its neighbour, Montepulciano D'Abruzzo. Characterful, vibrant, with lots of gutsy Italian spirit.

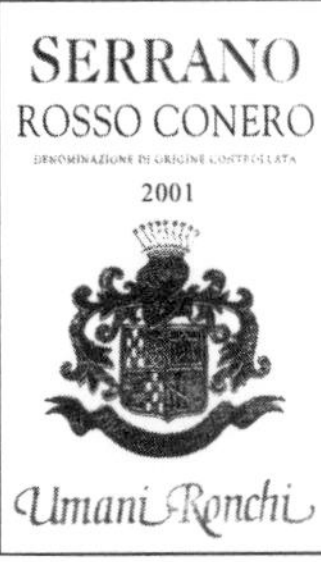

P.S. Italy's **Citra 2002 Montepulciano D'Abruzzo** ($6.60) and **Cesari 2002 Merlot** ($6.60) could be added to this lineup of burger reds.
See the Lively Red section in this book.

feel *good* **reds**

wines for ***mellow moods***

In the ***mood*** *for a fireside red.*

What a treat it is to be able to buy red wines with deep, cuddly flavours for only ten or twelve bucks. Plan the night, pick up a few bottles and relax.

service

Serve at room temperature. Use a large glass.

food ideas

Simple grilled or roasted meats and vegetables.

Talus 2002 Shiraz, California (#605501 $11.95) has deep and delicious flavours as well as an appetizing bite. Californian sunshine with Italian-style gusto. Fun and lively.

KWV 2001 Roodeberg, South Africa (#7187 $11.95). This wine just keeps on getting better and this new vintage is right up there with the world's greatest everyday reds. A seductively flavoured, generous, warm-hearted wine to partner with similar feelings. Don't be afraid to use a little spice or heat.

Hardys 2001 'Nottage Hill' Shiraz, South East Australia (#375964 $12.45) is cheerful, fruity and a little sweet/spicy. Fun to drink anytime with almost any food. Lovely, lovely stuff. One of the few Aussie wines that never tires the palate – the sixth glasss is as delightful as the first one.

take me out to the bistro *a bit of an edge*

In the mood *for wines with a bite.*

All wines were rustic at one time. It used to be that smoothness was neither possible nor desirable. Imagine that. Anyone who's been to a French bistro knows that the bite in traditional French wines made from Cabernet and Merlot (Bordeaux) is the perfect match for a grilled steak or lamb chop. Our local wine from the same grapes works equally well.

service

Serve at room temperature. Use a large glass.

food ideas

Classic bistro foods using cheaper cuts of meat, cooked slowly – like lamb shanks or steak and frites. These wines need food.

Chateau Canada 2000 Bordeaux, France (#559468 $14.95) will feel a bit rustic and hearty for some, but get a steak or a roast of something on the table and the wine will really shine. Manly, assertive, gutsy red – not for the timid. Experience how Merlot used to taste before it became a movie star. You gotta like the Chateau name.

Chateau des Charmes 2001 Cabernet/Merlot, Niagara (#454991 $12.95) is manly, gutsy wine for the serious big appetite. Beef or lamb for sure. Good stuff.

Pelee Island 2002 Merlot, Ontario (#612622 $11.95) would also welcome a table laden with a hearty dish of lamb or beef. Rustic, plummy and very appetizing.

Pillitteri 2001 Cabernet/ Merlot, Niagara (#349191 $9.95) is really good, frank, everyday red wine. There is even some charm.

imagine being seduced by a $10 wine

hello mellow

In the mood *to be charmed. Red wine for a slow dinner.*

Today's best source for warm-hearted, seductive reds at everyday prices is not Australia or Chile, but the south of Italy. It is the most improved wine region in the world. Spain is also sending us the occasional ten dollar charmer.

service

Serve at room temperature. Use a large glass.

food ideas

Cook whatever makes you feel good.

Agricole Vallone 2000 Salice Salentino 'Vereto', Puglia, Italy (#471730 $9.65). A sort of Burgundy meets Tawny Port experience. Mellow stuff. Could be the most seductive ten dollar wine in the store. A big time charmer with feather-like delicacy. Wine for a nice slow dinner with a slow roasted something. Or just drink it when you're in the mood to go slow.

Pasqua 2001 Primitivo 'Terre Del Sole' Salentino, Puglia, Italy (#561928 $9.45) offers richness, charm and vitality – the Italian dance – *bellissimo!* The Primitivo grape is supposedly related to Californian Zinfandel, and the delicious ripe berry flavours in this wine certainly suggest this. Comforting, but lively too – a great combination. Try it with bold-flavoured food – Mediterranean or Californian style.

Osborne 2000 'Solaz' Tempranillo/ Cabernet, Spain (#610188 $9.45) offers the lovely sweet berry flavours of the Tempranillo grape alongside the appetizing bite of Cabernet. Mature, warm feelings. Wine for a romantic mood.

4 **trips to** Europe

flavours of a region

In the mood *for red wine with strong, regional character.*

Today most of the wines that we drink are mainly about grape flavours. But it wasn't always so. Traditionally, wine was an expression of a region, of a place. Sipping the wine took you somewhere. The wines opposite offer armchair trips to France, Italy, Portugal and Spain. Bon voyage.

service

Serve room temperature in a nice big glass.

food ideas

Hearty meals with red meat.

M. Chapoutier 2000 'Rasteau' Côtes du Rhône-Villages, France (#321539 $15.10) combines all the lovely Rhône spicy/earthy flavours with a seductive charm. A great ambassador for the Rhône experience. Grilled meats would be my choice but I have enjoyed this wine with almost everything and anything. It's so agreeable.

Sogrape 2000 Dao 'Duque De Viseu', Portugal (#546309 $12.65) is a nourishing comfort wine that also has a rustic country feeling. The flavours are hard to pin down. Mystery is good.

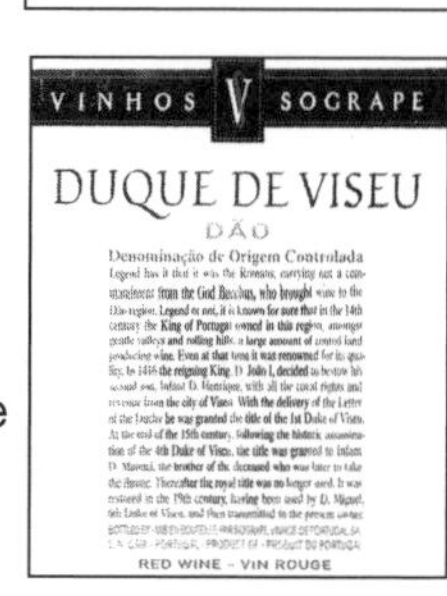

Bodegas Piqueras 2000 Castillo Almansa Reserva, Almansa, Spain (#270363 $9.95) is traditional, gutsy, earthy wine with heartwarming flavours. Manly stuff. Certainly a trip. Best new Spanish wine in years.

Duca Di Castelmonte 2000 Cent'are, Sicily, Italy (#546192 $12.50) offers power, flavour and charm. It's the current champion of Sicilian reds in our stores. Expect the feeling and fragrances of October in the woods – or meats roasted on the spit. But most of all, this wine is about Italian gusto. Great stuff for traditional pasta fare or roasted meats, but there is enough character for fancy dinners too.

a bit of *this* a bit of *that*

not mainstream ***but good***

In the mood *for a detour.*

The Chianti is invigorating, the Pinot is seductive and the Pelham wine is cheerful. Something for everyone.

service

The vitality in these wines will appear even brighter with a light chilling. Serve in a nice big glass.

food ideas

Hearty meals with red meat. Or whatever is going.

Brusco Dei Barbi 2000 Tuscany, Italy (#299073 $13.40) has bright, pure flavours – feels very natural. As invigorating as a brisk walk on a fall day. High spirited wine that really sets up your palate. Great with pasta or a roasted bird. Lightly chill.

Rocca Delle Macie 2001 Chianti Classico, Tuscany, Italy (#741769 $18.50) is nourishing. Woodsy and invigorating, it suggests something roasting on the spit – beef or lamb. The Johnny Cash of red wine – dramatic, unpretentious and very real.

Fetzer 2001 Pinot Noir 'Valley Oaks', California (#425447 $15.95) is a bit of a lush but the spicy/sweet flavours and silky texture are very seductive. Very Middle Eastern. Very romantic. Fantastic with herbed (cumin) chicken or salmon. Lightly chill.

Henry of Pelham 2002 Cabernet/Merlot 'Meritage', Niagara (#504241 $14.95) has the richish, plummy character associated with these grapes but vitality and cheerfulness play a big part too. A wine for lively times – maybe white meat rather than dark.

F FRESH WHITE
L LIVELY RED
M MEDIUM WHITE
M MEDIUM RED
R RICH WHITE
R RICH RED

for comfort and mellow moods
for substantial meals or for sipping

the heavyweights

- **The rich feeling.**
- **Excess.**
- **Glorious, big flavours.**
- **Slow-paced and expansive.**
- **These wines are big in flavour and richness – but not energy. They welcome a slow pace and some attention.**

food pairing: *seafood, chicken in a rich sauce, BBQ'd white meats, well-seasoned chicken or pork.*

watchpoint: *Good glassware will echo the sense of luxury and glamour in these wines. Refrigerated open bottles will keep well for 3 to 4 days.*

local **riches**

special occasion Chardonnays

In the mood *for a slow-paced dinner with a rich chicken or seafood dish. A mellow mood.*

Barrel fermentation imparts a toasty, spicy flavour in whites. It makes the wine feel creamy, rich and heartwarming. Lovely stuff for slow, relaxing dinners.

service

Serve cold – but not icy cold – in fine stemware.

food ideas

Find a recipe for herbed chicken or grilled salmon and polish up some nice glassware. Use ginger and Indian spices if you want an exotic focus.

Henry of Pelham 2002 Chardonnay 'Barrel Fermented', Niagara (#268342 $18.95). Full-blown Chardonnay flavour and heft. No Canadian politeness here. For a slow dinner. May be the best big white in the store.

P.S. There are many local rich Chardonnays produced – but in limited quantities. They get sold directly at the winery. For some of the best, visit Chateau des Charmes, Hillebrand, Inniskillin, Jackson-Triggs, Lailey, Lenko, Malivoire, Peller Estates, Southbrook and 13th Street.

See the 'tour section' in the back of this book for more details. And page 111 for information on buying on-line.

***In the mood** for BBQ white wines. Rich whites that have a fondness for foods with a charred or roasted flavour. A good partner for turkey too.*

A tangy bite is important in rich wine. It makes the wine more appetizing and prevents the richness from tiring your senses. It also provides an edge in the same way that grilling or BBQ'ing adds a bitter edge to foods. You could say that these wines represent the 'manly side' of rich whites.

service

Seve cold – but not icy cold – in fine stemware.

food ideas

Anything you like to BBQ – shrimp, chicken, seafood. Cajun blackened chicken might be an equal match for the wine's intensity. Or drink with turkey at family holidays.

Simonsig 2001 Chardonnay, South Africa (#345389 $11.75) is the big sex show. Spicy, showy wine with flavours of tropical fruit
. . . and scotch. Honest. It's big 'n bold. Hot stuff for a hot affair with your grill. Fire up them coals.

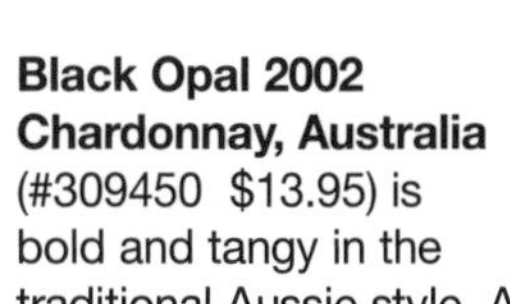

Black Opal 2002 Chardonnay, Australia (#309450 $13.95) is bold and tangy in the traditional Aussie style. A BBQ mate for sure.

Santa Rita 2003 Chardonnay '120', Chile (#315184 $8.75) has a raunchy, masculine character – invigorating, tangy, go for the gusto wine. A big expansive wine at a budget price.

Wolf Blass 2002 Chardonnay, Australia (#226860 $14.95) has a lively lemon tang to contrast the delicious exotic fruit flavours. Not the biggest show on earth but a good workhorse.

Louis Jadot 2000 Bourgogne Chardonnay, France (#933077 $19.95) goes deep in the flavour end – with a lift, heft and solidness. Manly, appetizing Chardonnay for a well-seasoned and charred chicken or chop.

lovely
but not loud
understated richness

In the mood *for a dinner party wine that won't try to upstage your food or friends.*

Here's a few rich whites that don't flaunt their excess. Talented but not showy. The 'Buicks' of Chardonnay.

service

Serve cold – but not icy cold – in fairly fancy stemware.

food ideas

Any seafood or white meat that calls out for white wine. Scallops perhaps.

Santa Rita 2002 Chardonnay 'Reserva', Chile (#348359 $11.65). Flavourful, rich, lively. It has it all. And at an attractive price. This has consistently been one of the best values in rich whites since I started publishing this annual handbook.

Wynns Connawarra 2001 Chardonnay, Australia (#468728 $14.90) is an elegant wine with great vitality. Dinner party white, but a joy to sip without food too.

Sebastiani 2000 Chardonnay Sonoma, California (#361635 $12.85) has developed mature flavours – feels very rich, warming, and mellow. Wine for a slow evening.

rich *red*

for comfort and mellow moods
for substantial meals or for sipping

the heavyweights

- **The rich feeling.**
- **Excess.**
- **Glorious, big flavours.**
- **Slow paced and expansive.**
- **These wines are big in flavour and richness – but not energy. They welcome a slow pace and require some attention.**

food pairing: *steak, lamb, roasts, rich braised meats.*

watchpoint: *Good glassware will echo the sense of luxury and glamour in these wines.*

merry **merlot**

the champion of richness

In the mood *for a rich red.*

When it comes to selecting the world's favourite red, it's a toss up between Merlot and Shiraz. Merlot fans will argue that it has a greater range of styles and uses, and that it's more elegant. It certainly can be voluptuous, as you'll discover when you try the wines opposite.

service

Serve in large glasses at room temperature.

food ideas

Go big or stay home.

Robert Skalli 2001 Merlot VDP d'Oc, France (#571042 $13.00) is full of warmth and richness. The 'Full Monty' of Merlots. Big time jammy, spicy/sweet flavours. Plan the big night. Porterhouse perhaps. Produced by the Fortant de France guy.

Familia Rutini 2002 Merlot 'Trumpeter', Argentina (#467985 $13.30) is not for the lighthearted. A huge, beefy, hefty red that needs the steak and candles evening. Manly wine.

Concha Y Toro 2002 Merlot 'Casillero Del Diablo', Chile (#427088 $10.90) is a plummy, solid Merlot. Great winter nourishment. And a great value.

Grant Burge 2001 Merlot, Barossa, Australia (#627182 $16.45) has the ripe, peppery flavours associated with Shiraz. Earthy, quite solid and tangy. Needs grilled or roasted red meat.

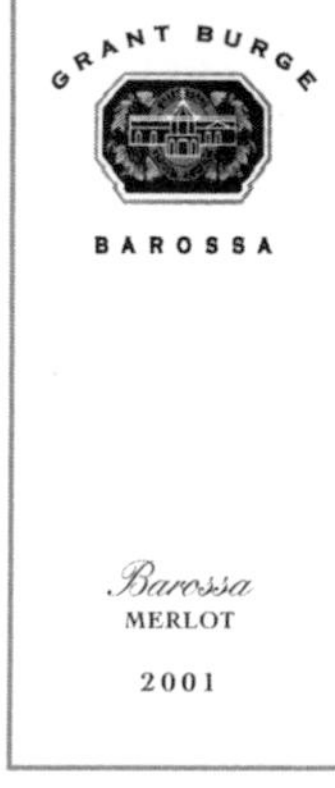

cabernet
time

the traditional **power wine**

In the mood *for a red that will make you feel like an emperor.*

Cabernet Sauvignon was once the cornerstone of red wine because it had the greatest presence – it made the biggest statement. And it was serious. Cabernet was always poured at state functions. But drinkers have discovered big reds that are friendlier and more fun, so Cabernet is going through a personality crisis. It's becoming less serious. The wines opposite reflect some old and some new styles.

service

Serve in large glasses.

food ideas

Think big and powerful – steak or lamb.

Wynns 2000 Cabernet Sauvignon, Coonawarra, Australia (#502039 $18.95) is traditional, solid, serious and powerfully concentrated. It has great vitality for such a rich wine. Decant, grill a steak, put on a suit and you'll be all set.

Santa Rita 2001 Cabernet Sauvignon Reserve, Chile (#253872 $11.80) is modern-style, friendly Cabernet. And awfully good. You'll find richness, tons of flavours, a solid centre, charm and an all round feeling of warmth. Very generous but not gushy wine. Good enough for dinner parties, fun enough for a burger bash. Sensational value.

Vinas Del Vero 2000 Cabernet Sauvignon Somontano, Spain (#499169 $11.95) starts out terribly serious in the classic Bordeaux style (the region is on the French border) but a little Latin spirit creeps in later. Another great value. Best to think bistro foods with this one, roast beef or lamb.

the ripassos

(no relation to the Sopranos)

sexy Italians

In the mood *for rich red wine with old-fashioned charm.*

The Valpolicella region in the north of Italy is best known for inexpensive, light reds to drink with pizza, and for a rich, hedonistic wine called Amarone. An in-between style of red, called Ripasso, is also produced and it's awfully good. And reasonably priced.

Ripassos are drier and more appetizing than most rich reds. They are great partners for a broad range of foods, from Italian tomato sauced foods, to fowl and even steak.

service

Serve in large glasses.

food ideas

Red meats – steak, lamb, sausages, pheasant, or hearty chicken dishes with roasted vegetables. Or no food – just sip it alone or with cheese.

Serego Alighieri 2000 Valpolicella Classico, Italy (#447326 $15.00) starts out slowly, but nourishing richness and belly-warming, woodsy and old world flavours settle in later. Soulful. So good on a winter's night with a roast.

Bertani 2000 Valpolicella Secco, Italy (#12443 $15.50) is the delicate, shy one in the group. Or so it appears at first – it becomes a charmer later. A delicious partner for a roasted bird.

Pasqua 2000 'Sagramoso' Ripasso Valpolicella, Italy (#602342 $15.85) is hugely concentrated, rich and seductive. Glamour wine. Almost giddy in its exuberance – great company on a winter's evening.

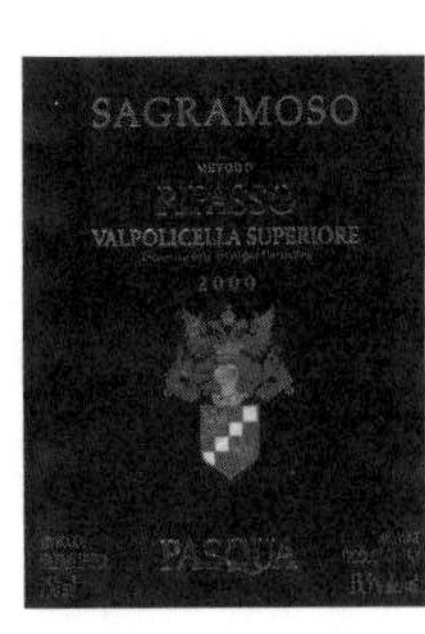

Cesari 2000 'Mara' Ripasso Valpolicella, Italy (#506519 $14.85) is the smooth, soft, mellow, sweet member of the family. A crowd-pleaser for sure.

heavy seduction

Hollywood style

In the mood *for comfort drinks.*

This is the page for those who like 'em big. These are high alcohol, super-rich reds that closely resemble Port. There is a cuddly warmth and mellow sweetness that's mighty seductive. Traditionally, this style of wine was reserved for banquets, but now it is common to indulge in them more frequently – even daily. Rich reds have become our comfort drink.

service

Serve at room temperature – always in a big glass.

food ideas

Enjoy with or without food.

Cline 2000 Syrah, California (#733758 $17.95) is a fuller Syrah than the Phillips. Great warmth and richness – wine for the big chill out. You'll not be going out after a bottle of this. But you'll feel awfully good.

R.H. Philips 2000 Syrah, Dunnigan Hills, California (#576272 $16.55) is the Californian edition of Chateauneuf-Du-Pape – big, rich and spicy. Vibrant and appetizing too. An invitation to have fun. Think spicy/sweet Californian cuisine and a sunset.

Cline 2001 Zinfandel, California (#489278 $16.30) is Port-like in richness. Tons of spicy/sweet flavours. Very sensual. Suggests the fireside, Christmas Day and romance. Your choice.

Ravenswood 2001 Zinfandel, California (#359257 $19.95) is a solid, manly, earthy version of the above. Big time nourishment. The driest tasting wine in this group. Fabulous with any hearty food. Ravenswood is a cult figure in Californian Zin.

shir-az-nice

the crowd-pleaser

In the mood *for wine that's as nourishing and seductive as chocolate. A big red for a big steak or burger.*

Aussie Shiraz is a big hit because it fulfills our desire for instant gratification with its softness, smoothness and sweet/chocolate flavours. As someone once said, "Shiraz tastes like Christmas Day." The experience of Shiraz can be similar to the in-your-face character of popular entertainment today. Little is left to the imagination, there is no buildup, there is no mystery – you get it all right away. And you get lots.

I've selected wines that I think are the most food friendly – and which won't exhaust your senses. At least for the first hour.

service

Serve at room temperature – in the biggest glass you have.

food ideas

Enjoy with or without food.

Hardys 'Crest' 2000 Cabernet/Shiraz/ Merlot, Australia (#565119 $15.15) is a 'best of all worlds' wine, offering the cuddly warmth of Shiraz alongside a playful personality. Capable of being fancy or just-for-fun. A lively Shiraz.

Houghton 2001 Shiraz, West Australia (#338673 $16.00) has a fresh, bright, fruit character because it's from Australia's cooler climate wine region. The big flavours of Shiraz are coupled with an invigorating tang – Aussie Baco! Great for stimulating the appetite. Enjoy with well-seasoned grilled meats. Not a party wine.

P.S. Wolf Blass and Rosemount are the big sellers in this category but their wines are a bit tight and raw, or just plain. Not good value.

The Aussie Wine Families

Part of the driving force behind the Aussie wine boom is its big wineries. And the consolidation of its big wineries. Lindemans, Penfolds, Rosemount and Wynns are all part of the same corporation. Wolf Blass recently merged with Beringer of California. And Hardys got into bed with Constellation Brands (US) making them the world's largest wine company. Each winery, however, does retain a house style and here's how I see them:

***Hardys:** fruity, friendly, spreading good cheer*
***Lindemans:** fun, lighthearted, party wine*
***Penfolds:** traditional, the French school, dinner wine*
***Rosemount:** correct, corporate, wine in suits*
***Wolf Blass:** lush, spicy, seductive*

Gourgazaud *Guigal* + **Montalcino**

the ***final three*** *reds*

In the mood *for rich reds.*

Minervois is in the French Languedoc region, which has become France's new wine world. The past decade has seen an amazing make-over and now Languedoc's vineyard size is twice that of Australia's – and just as modern. And every bit as sunny, as Languedoc is located in the extreme south. The focus is mainly on good every-day wine, and lots of it. While the wines have hot climate ripeness, they tend to be less over-the-top than Aussie wine.

Mr. Guigal makes some of the best rich reds in the Rhône region and his wine has been in my book since the beginning. Tuscany is not known for richness but the wine opposite may change that.

service

Serve at room temperature – in a big glass.

food ideas

Enjoy with traditional bistro foods – chicken, pork, beef or game.

Ch. De Gourgazaud 2002 Minervois, France (#22384 $10.95). Delicious peppery, smokey, plummy flavours (Syrah and Mourvedre grapes) are combined with the frank and appetizing character of traditional French wines. Lots of character. I particularly like the youthful vitality at this stage.

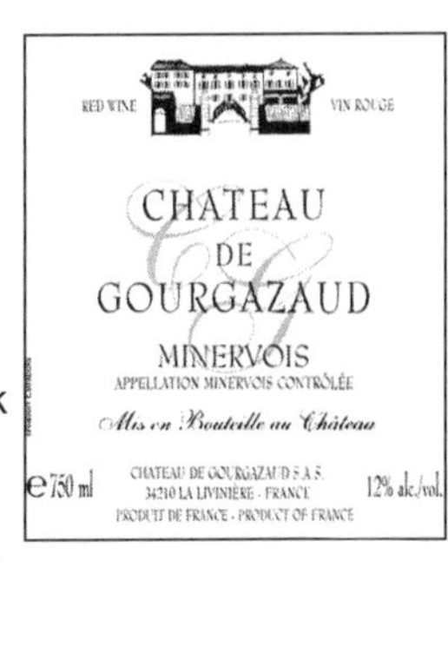

E. Guigal 2000 Côtes du Rhône, France (#259721 $17.20) is the daddy of the Rhône wines in our stores. The richest and the most masculine. Substantial stuff. A firm handshake. But in the spirit of Cary Grant – elegant and sexy. Beef with this one.

Frescobaldi 2001 Rosso Di Montalcino 'Campo Ai Sassi', Tuscany, Italy (#201855 $15.95). Ripe, rich and nourishing. Very much in the modern out-to-please style. A good winter warmer.
P.S. Montalcino is a neighbour of Chianti and the wines are similar, but richer.

fringe *wines*

for sipping & celebrating

- Extra easy.
- Extra sweet.
- Extra strong.
- The miscellaneous.

aromatic
not-so-dry
party, patio or garden wines

In the mood *for easy-sipping.*

Summer is the best season to enjoy this 'aromatic' category of wines because of their garden-like flavours and lighthearted feeling, and because the low alcohol allows for serious gulping. They're especially good on any deck or dock, and with Sunday brunch. Not-so-dry wines offer a change of pace, which is what seasons are all about. Serve all these wines quite cold because that will emphasize their zest and balance their fruity sweetness.

service
Serve in fun, narrow glassware. Colourful and casual is good.

food ideas
Brunch menu items, lunch salads, summer dishes.

Good cheer and liveliness is the message in **Cave Spring 2001 Off-Dry Riesling, Niagara** (#234583 $11.25). Refreshing as well as tasty. Great lunch wine.

Pelee Island 2002 Gewurztraminer, Ontario (#326413 $8.95) is off-dry and easy to take on a lazy summer's afternoon. Good party wine too.

Bodegas Jacques & François Lurton 2002 Pinot Gris, Mendoza, Argentina (#556746 $9.20) is super-nice, super-pleasant, and would be a great choice for lazy-time sipping. The slight sweetness is a good partner for egg dishes.

A medium-dry sparkling is a good idea for parties because not everyone likes bone-dry wines. **Martini & Rossi's Demi-Sec, Italy** (#415372 $10.80) is clean and refreshing with not a trace of sweet aftertaste.

Sogrape 'Mateus Rosé', Portugal (#166 $7.40) has been reborn in a drier style and I suggest that you give it another chance. This is no longer the frivolous stuff of old, but a decent everyday refresher or party drink. A slight spritz adds to the fun and the smart new package is graceful enough for the fanciest condo.

sweet *little bottles*

In the mood for something sweet.

These wines taste equally good in the winter or on a hot, sultry summer evening. The flavours are wonderful and some are as refreshing as they are sweet. The current selection is not great but there are a few very good buys. Those living in major centres should visit a Vintages store or boutique for a better selection.

service

I like to drink these wines cold because it tempers the sweetness. Opened bottles will keep well for a week stored in the fridge. Serve in small, sherry-style glasses.

food ideas

Chocolate anything with the Framboise, and biscotti, almond or lemon cake, or apple crisp with the others.

Colio Estates 2001 Late Harvest Vidal, Ontario (#470369 375 ml/$9.95) is a great value.Wonderful honey and peach flavours are balanced with a nutty tang. Enjoy with biscotti or an almond cake.

Cave Spring 2000 Select Late Harvest Riesling 'Indian Summer', Niagara (#415901 375ml/$21.95) is a wonderful mix of tropical flavours and freshness. It's an uplifting feeling – really fills the mouth – but there is not a trace of sweetness in the aftertaste. Enjoy with cake or just on its own.

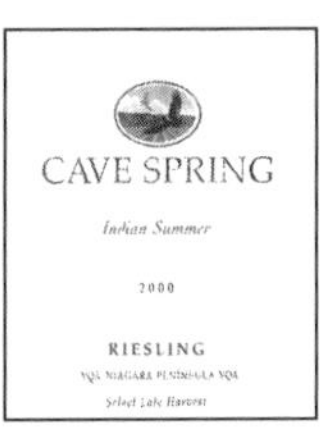

While the initial sensation of **Henry of Pelham 2000 Special Select Late Harvest Vidal, Niagara** (#395228 375ml/$18.95) is luscious with sweet, peachy flavours, this wine also has a light and zesty character. It's as refreshing as it is sweet. The ideal little sip for after a summer lunch in the garden, or late evening on the porch, or 'whenever'.

Southbrook Winery Framboise, Ontario (#341024 375ml/$14.45) is a liqueur-like wine made from raspberries. Try this one with your favourite chocolate dessert. Or just pour over ice cream.

a glass of **port**

strong, sweet stuff

***In the mood** for a heartwarming drink.*

The Port section is very strong again this year, even if it's mainly the same gang as last time. I suggest you buy a little stash and discover the difference between the Tawny and Vintage styles. Simply put, the former is feminine and the latter is masculine. For the best examples of each, get the charming Graham's 10-Year-Old Tawny and the fiery, manly Taylor Fladgate LBV. You can have lots of fun deciding which one is right for your mood. Port continues to be one of the great values in wine when you consider the age, flavour, concentration and overall character of what you're buying. Get some and celebrate cold winter nights.

P.S. The world of **Vintage Port** is something that most of us can live without. As with Grand Cru wines, you pay lots ($75+), need to cellar it for years and probably never find the time or the company worthy of the wine. The Ports I'm recommending are ready to drink tonight, and are affordable enough to drink every night.

service

Serve in small, elegant sherry/port glasses.

food ideas

Nuts and cheese. But great just alone.

Rich fruitiness and charm are the features in **Deleforce Rich Tawny, Portugal** (#154807 $14.20). More Ruby than Tawny, but a lovely anytime drink for everyday pleasure.

Taylor Fladgate 1997 Late Bottle Vintage, Portugal (#46946 $17.75) and **Fonseca Bin 27 Port, Portugal** (#156877 $15.55) are powerfully concentrated and rich with lots of fire in the belly. Manly stuff to have at the end of a big meal. Certainly mates for Stilton.

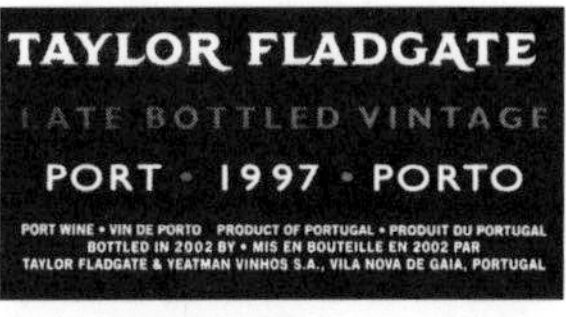

Graham's 10-Year-Old Tawny, Portugal (#206508 $27.95) is an exciting mix of fire and silky texture. A great Tawny Port experience for the price.

a glass of **sherry**

dry is best

In the mood *for a strong wine.*

Most of the Sherries that you see have been doctored (think smooth and sweet) for mass appeal. The real thing is a bold, challenging drink with all the character and flavour interest of Single Malt Scotch. And it's mostly bone dry. Real Sherry is hard to find – if you're interested, I suggest you talk to a product consultant at a Vintages store. Ask about dry Oloroso or Amontillado.

There is one classic style available, however, and it's called Fino. This is the lightest and driest Sherry.

service

Serve cold. Pour about 2 ounces in a small sherry or port glass.

food ideas

Think seafood, and Spain.

Producer Gonzalez Byass has dumped the traditional black garb and re-outfitted its **Tio Pepe Fino** in a fresh, green package. Same bone-dry, crisp, refreshing drink but it's amazing how much more appeal it has now. Fino is a high alcohol (about 15%) dry wine so it packs a punch. A tang. It's a great hot weather aperitif or partner for shrimps on the BBQ. A little Fino goes a long way so it's quite the bargain. A refrigerated open bottle keeps well for at least a week.
Gonzalez Byass Fino 'Tio Pepe', Spain
(#242669 $14.95)

P.S. **William & Humber 'Dry Sack', Spain** (#13565 $12.00) is one of the better commercial Sherries. A pleasant, medium-dry, anytime sipper. Chill well. It also has been re-outfitted with a new look.

Find price and vintage updates of the wines recommended in this book in the handbook section of www.billysbestbottles.com.

Hire us
for your next party!

My partner, Kato Wake and I can host a **wine tasting in your home for you and 10 (or more) of your friends.** My **'one hour wine expert course' costs $35 per person** and **includes the wines** (3 whites and 3 reds which will be blind tasted), **a copy of this wonderful book, and us! The host is free.** It's a great way to experience my **'Wine Spectrum' in action** – and is more fun than a tupperware party. A travel allowance (45¢ km.) will be added for visits outside Toronto. The wine tasting takes about 2 hours – so you can organize a pot luck dinner or cook for your friends after we leave.

"The quality has never been better, but many people still shy away because they find wine too confusing and intimidating. My seminar is designed to help the novice become more comfortable and confident with wine. Everyone has the ability to taste, they just have not been given the freedom to express their wine experiences in a way that's imaginative, personal and meaningful."

Sound good? For more details, see the 'events/workshops' section of **www.billysbestbottles.com.**

Want more?

We have more!

. . . for the enthusiast

If you have enjoyed this book, chances are you'll also enjoy **Billy's Best Bottles Wineletter**. It comes out **six times a year** and contains **40 pages of reviews** of all the new wines as they arrive at the LCBO. Each issue is jammed with dozens of **hot tips about wines (mainly under $15), lots of useful information** and **wine chat**. You'll also find a smattering of my restaurant and bar selections and occasional beer reviews. The **best buys from LCBO Vintages Stores** are also offered along with a **handy shopping list of 100 current wines** and the issue's **best picks 'wine cards'**.

Billy's Best Bottles is **Canada's original consumer wine buying guide** – in its 21st year, with subscribers in every province. **It is not sold in stores, has no advertisers and is supported solely by reader's subscriptions.** If you are **seriously interested in independent, comprehensive reviews on wines** (as opposed to paid positioned advertising under the guise of 'wine information') please consider subscribing. You will be rewarded with a publication that goes the extra mile to give you **information with integrity and passion.** Not to mention **great savings – and better wine – every time you go shopping.**

See the other side for details. *We'd be pleased to send a you a trial issue.*

buying *wine*

LCBO

LCBO Vintages

Buying Wine On-Line

Private Wine Stores

At the Wineries

- *Beamsville*
- *Niagara-on-the-Lake*
- *Lake Erie North Shore*
- *Toronto*

Wine Events Calendar

buying *wine at the* **LCBO**

The Eight Biggies: There are eight stores that stock all LCBO wines:

Kitchener 324 Highland Road 519.745.8781
London 71 York Street 519.432.1831
Toronto
> Queen's Quay & Cooper St. 416.864.6777
> Crossroads, Weston Rd. & Hwy. 401 416.243.3320
> Bayview & Sheppard Avenues 416.222.7658
> 1123 Yonge Street 416.922.2924
Ottawa 1980 Bank Street 613.523.7763
Windsor 3155 Howard Avenue 519.967.1772

Your Local Store: Don't be disappointed if you cannot find my recommendations at your local store. Simply ask the staff to order them in by the bottle or case. Or visit www.lcbo.com and search for product/store stocks.

LCBO Infoline: You can get information on wine availability at any store by calling the LCBO Infoline. In Toronto, call 416.365.5900. Elsewhere you can call toll-free at 1.800.ONT.LCBO. The lines are open 9 a.m. to 6 p.m., Monday to Saturday.

Price Changes: Because wine is produced by thousands of individuals under different conditions in thousands of different parts of the world, its price will tend to fluctuate more than the price of toothpaste. Prices given in this book are those at press time, but some may change by the time you shop.

Find price and vintage updates of the wines recommended in this book in the handbook section of www.billysbestbottles.com.

buying *at the LCBO* VINTAGES

The board created this separate division to sell drinks that were not available in the quantities necessary to supply its six hundred LCBO stores. Vintages stores operate like a market in that new wines arrive on the shelves twice a month and when they're sold, they're gone. The ratio of good to boring wines is about the same at Vintages as at regular LCBOs – one in ten. Their beautiful monthly catalogue tries hard to make you believe otherwise. While one can get along quite nicely without Vintages wine, I recommend it to anyone with the enthusiasm for more variety.

Vintages locations:

Toronto

> Queen's Quay & Cooper St. 416.864.6777

> 2901 Bayview Ave., Bayview Village Mall 416.222.7658

Mississauga

> 1900 Dundas St. W., Sherwood Forrest Mall 905.823.4524

Ottawa 275 Rideau Street 613.789.5226

All the bigger LCBOs carry a selection of Vintages wines.

P.S. Vintages also publishes a catalogue of 'classic' wines. Just about all the great drinks in the world (including Cognac, Scotch, Port, etc.) are offered. Older bottles and large format bottles make great gifts. You can order by phone, have your order shipped to your local store and pay by credit card.

Fans of local wine can shop at home thanks to **www.winerytohome.com**. Many Niagara wineries are participating and you can search for products via the wine name or food pairing. Shipping charges are a dollar a bottle in Toronto but more for the rest of the province. Many interesting local wines never hit the LCBO shelves, so this service provides new opportunities for both the buyer and the seller.

buying
wine at the
OTHER STORES

The Wine Rack, The Wine Shoppe, and Colio Wine Boutiques (located mainly in supermarkets) are worth visiting because they offer a few excellent wines not available at LCBOs. And it's fun to shop elsewhere. Call for the locations nearest to you.

THE WINE RACK
(Inniskillin, Jackson-Triggs and Sawmill Creek)
1.800.265.9463 www.winerack.com
Fans of Riesling and Cabernet should not miss this pair of fantastic wines:

> **Jackson-Triggs 2001 Riesling 'Delaine Vineyards'** ($15.95)
> **Inniskillin 1999 Meritage** ($16.95)

THE WINE SHOPPE/VINEYARDS
(Hillebrand + Peller Esates)
1.800.230.4321 www.winecountryathome.com

> **Hillebrand 'Vineyard Select' 2002 Pinot Gris** ($10.95)
> **Peller Estates 2002 Dry Riesling 'Private Reserve'** ($14.95)
> **Peller Estates 2000 Cabernet Franc 'Private Reserve'** ($19.85)

The Pinot Gris is a delightful, lazy-time or after work sipper and the Riesling is a classic aperitif or wine for fish. Pair the Cabernet Franc with any grilled meat. Vineyards stores in Niagara-on-the-Lake and at 3143 Yonge Street in Toronto provide upscale urban retail experiences, and the company's on-line shopping is also smartly run.

COLIO WINE BOUTIQUES
1.800.265.1322 or 519.738.2231
www.coliowinery.com
Colio Estates Vineyards (CEV) wines have generous flavours and great drinkability. Try the spicy Cabernet Franc listed below with fowl or game.

> **Colio Estates 2000 Cabernet Franc** ($19.95)

If you are not familiar with the Niagara region I'd like to point out that there are two distinct wine areas: the BEAMSVILLE BENCH, which is west of St. Catharines, and NIAGARA-ON-THE-LAKE, which is at the tip of the Peninsula. It's best to choose just one area unless you are spending a few days. Beamsville has more small wineries and the best views – but nobody should miss seeing the new Jackson-Triggs winery, which is close to Niagara-on-the-Lake.

Beamsville area

from Grimsby to St. Catharines along Regional Road #81

Peninsula Ridge Estates *(Regional Road 81, Grimsby)*
Spectacular restoration of an estate farm. High-end wines and a high-end restaurant. A showpiece.
905.563.0900 www.peninsularidge.com

Malivoire Winery *(Regional Road 81, Beamsville)*
Tasteful, modern/west coast-style winery. Distinctive, concentrated, rich wines.
905.563.9253 www.malivoirewineco.com

Eastdell Estates *(4041 Locust Lane, Beamsville)*
Good everyday wines. Very popular destination because

>>>continued

GOOD EARTH COOKING SCHOOL

While in the Beamsville area I highly recommend a cooking class at the Good Earth. Nestled among beautiful gardens on a 55-acre fruit farm, the school offers many different classes as well as seasonal special events. There is a fully equipped outdoor kitchen for summer events. All their classes are limited to 12 'foodies' who enjoy cooking, eating and fun. Call Nicolette Novak at *905.563.7856 or 1.800.308.5124. www.goodearthcooking.com*

of its casualness and the views from the café/restaurant. Feels like you're visiting someone's cottage.
905.563.WINE www.eastdell.com

Vineland Estates *(3620 Meyer Road, Vineland)*
Niagara's best located winery – you're bound to be impressed. High-end restaurant. Riesling for aging is their speciality.
905.562.7088 www.vineland.com.

A NEW BREAD HAVEN

Stratford Chef School grads Heather and Lenny Karmiol have settled in Vineland (on the wine route) and have opened a bakery and catering co. called Vinehaven. Their artisan breads are baked in a wood-fired oven and are made from organic, stone-ground flours (no chemicals or additives) and natural 'sourdough' culture. Real bread! Having world-class restaurant training experience (California, Italy, Japan) this duo also offers cooking classes and catering services for parties and events. You can buy their breads at selected organic markets in Toronto and Hamilton, or stop by at their house, see the oven and stock up for your picnic.
Vinehaven Catering & Bakery, 3543 King Street, Vineland (opposite Kacaba Winery) 905.562.9333

Cave Spring Cellars *(Main Street, Jordan)*
Good taste in everything, including the huge restaurant and deluxe accommodations across the street. A spa too. A great showpiece. Lunch here, perhaps, or have an early dinner at the end of the day. Or just a cold beer. A good touring base. Top-rated Chardonnay, Riesling, Gamay and Cabernet. A full service winery for sure.
905.562.3581 www.cavespringcellars.com

Henry of Pelham *(1469 Pelham Road, St. Catharines)*
Cozy, friendly pub atmosphere in this former coach inn. Casual café featuring Canadian cheeses. Interesting family collection of contemporary Canadian art. Traditional, hands-on family winery with a talented winemaker. One of Niagara's best for sure. Chardonnay, Riesling, Sauvignon Blanc, Baco Noir, Cabernet and Merlot. And a fantastic

Brut Sparkling 'Cuvee Catharine'.
905.684.8423 www.henryofpelham.com

Creekside Estates *(2170 Fourth Avenue, Jordan Station)*
Not much to look at, but there's good Sauvignon Blanc, Riesling and Pinot Noir. High-end.
905.562.0033 www.creeksideestatewinery.com

13th Street Wine Co. *(3983 13th Street, Jordan Station)*
Two small wineries in one: G.H. FUNK and SANDSTONE. Very high quality wines, especially Riesling, Gamay, Pinot Noir and Sparkling. Open Saturdays only. *905.562.9463*

For wine region maps visit
www.winesofontario.org

Niagara-on-the-Lake area

Hillebrand Winery *(Highway 55, Virgil)*
Big place, can be busy, but tastings and tours are conducted by well-trained staff. Great range of wines with quality at all levels. Large restaurant – one of the best in Niagara. Patio overlooking the vineyards. Tons of events. Worth checking out.
905.468.7123 or 1.800.582.8412
www.hillebrand.com

Jackson-Triggs *(Highway 55, Niagara-on-the-Lake)*
Modern spin on the traditional barn design. Fantastic space for the production of wine, for tasting it, and for enjoying the vineyard vistas. A refreshing break from *ye olde* look – a must visit. Take a tour and check out the outdoor amphitheatre. Café eats. Excellent mid-range and everyday wines, many recommended in this book.
905.468.4637 www.jacksontriggswinery.com

Peller Estates *(290 John Street, Niagara-on-the-Lake)*
Chateau grandeur in keeping with historic homes on the same street. Very much the country manor,

complete with elegant restaurant overlooking the vineyards. A lovely lunch stop. Patio too. One of the smartest tasting rooms in Niagara. Full range of wines, from charming 'Private Reserve' Riesling ($12), right up to the impressive 'Signature Series' Cabernet Sauvignon ($44).
905.468.4678 www.peller.com

Strewn Winery *(1339 Lake Shore Rd., Niagara-on-the-Lake)*
Nice grounds and good mix of modern and old touches in this former canning factory. Fantastic Dry Riesling with several past years still available. Good Cabernet Franc too. The on-site *La Cachette* restaurant serves quality French Bistro food and feels quite relaxing compared to places in town. There is a cooking school too.
905.468.1229 www.strewnwinery.com

NIAGARA COLLEGE TEACHING WINERY

Niagara College's winemaking course is for real. Students make real wine and it's sold at the college's retail store. None of this might be of much interest to you if it weren't for the fact that Niagara's winemaking legend, Jim Warren (formerly of Stoney Ridge), is one of the main instructors. The wines have won gold and silver metals in competitions and sell out quickly because there's not much made. Try their Sauvignon Blanc, Cabernet Franc and Chardonnay – if there's some available.
Niagara College Teaching Winery, Glendon Campus, 135 Taylor Road (opposite White Oak's Resort)
905.641.2252 ext.4070 www.winedec.com

Lailey Vineyard *(15940 Niagara Pkwy., Niagara-on-the-Lake)*
Donna and David Lailey have been growers for over thirty years but only recently opened their own winery. The wines are made by Derek Barnett, who has vaulted Lailey into the top-five category of local wineries. Some of the best Pinot Noir, Cabernet Franc and Merlot wines to be had in Ontario. In the $25-$35 price range. A new experiment aging wines in Ontario Oak casks has impressive results.
905.468.0503 www.laileyvineyard.com

Prince Edward County

'The County' is getting lots of publicity and one might expect to find some Tuscan wonderland with vineyards and villas at every turn of the road. It will be a few years yet. Look for a winery tour in my 2005 edition.

the southwest Lake Erie North Shore

This is Canada's most southerly vineyard district. It stretches between Leamington and Amherstburg, but it is best known for Pelee Island. The region enjoys a 2 to 3 week longer growing season than Niagara. My sources tell me that things are on the upswing and that we should expect several new wineries to open soon. Apparently there has been lots of planting in the past five years.

Colio Estates Winery *(1 Colio Drive, Harrow)*
An attractive revamped winery and tasting room. The quality and value of Colio's everyday wines is one of the reasons I drink local wine. Winemaker Carlo Negri works a 'good drinkability' spirit into everything he produces. Try his Cabernet Franc with a rustic meal.
519.738.224 www.coliowines.com

Pelee Island Winery *(455 Seacliff, County Rd. 20, Kingsville)*
Reasonably priced, good everyday wines in attractive packaging have made Pelee one of the most successful wineries in Canada. The 'Vinedresser Series', a new line of premium wines, should prove to be another feather in their cap. The winery is on the mainland but there is a Wine Pavilion on the island offering food, entertainment and drink. It's a two hour ferry ride, or only 30 minutes on the new hydrofoil.
519.724.2469 www.peleeisland.com

Grape Tree Estates *(308 Mersea Road 3, Leamington)*
Former LCBO product consultant, Steve Brook, is

running two vineyards and producing some interesting wines, including a tasty sparkler, 'Hexagon', made from six grapes varieties. Steve is enthusiastic about the wines, the food, the culture and just about everything else in his region. Visit him.
519.322.2081 www.grapetreewines.com

Sanson Estate Winery *(9238 Walker Rd., McGregor – near Amherstburg)*
Dennis Sanson is a former chef and his winery is off to a fast start producing fantastic, zesty Sauvignon Blanc ($14.00) and blockbuster Baco Noir Reserve ($18.00). Smart-looking labels and retail shop too.
519.726.9609

Not far from Sanson is another modest new winery called **Erie Shore Vineyards**, operated by husband and wife team Harvey and Alma Holingshead. Well-tended vineyards and wines with lovely pure flavours. Baco is good here too, as is Cabernet Franc Rosé. Both are on the austere side.
519.738.9858 www.erieshore.ca

*P.S. If you're down this way be sure to visit the pretty town of Amherstburg and **Caldwell's Grant restaurant**. Modern food in an old tavern – shades of New Orleans. 519.736.2100*

Toronto area

All four of Toronto's wineries are located close to each other in the northeast corner of the city, which goes by various names such as Vaughan, Maple and Woodbridge. Maybe they will simplify it one day and just call the area 'Wineland'. All are open Sundays.

Magnotta Winery *(271 Chrislea Road, Woodbridge)*
Magnotta offers a huge range of drinks at prices ten to twenty percent lower than the LCBO's. A big seller is its icewine, in a distinctive blue bottle. Magnotta's headquarters are as big and wonderful as a New York art gallery – and so unexpected in

this discount warehouse suburb of T.O. A winegarden is open in summer, and the huge cellars beneath the store are available for private functions. Call for the locations of other stores.
905.738.WINE or 1.800.461.9463
www.magnotta.com

Southbrook Winery *(1061 Major Mackenzie Drive, Richmond Hill)*
Southbrook's Bill Redelmeier is having fun producing local versions of Burgundy and Bordeaux in old farm buildings just north of Toronto. Framboise has been the big success to date, but Chardonnay, Sauvignon Blanc, Pinot Noir and Cabernet have hit high spots too. Check out the 'Triomphus' wines. Many wine events are held during the summer. Southbrook also has a huge roadside produce shop.
905.832.2548 www.southbrook.com

Vinotecca Winery *(527 Jevlan Drive, Woodbridge)*
Owners Giovanni and Rosanna Follegot see themselves as a winery for the family – making wine at prices people want to pay. Lots of everyday wines, some wine for celebrations and a little fancy stuff. They sell Niagara/Italy blends for $6.95. Chardonnay and Cabernet sold under the 'reserve' label are rich, ripe and flavourful.
905.856.5700 www.toronto.com/vinoteca

Cilento Winery *(627 Chrislea Road, Woodbridge)*
Like its neighbours, Cilento grew out of the juice-for-wine business. Thirty acres have been planted in Niagara and this ultra-smart winery displays a serious commitment to local wine. Best wines so far have been Riesling, Cabernet Franc and a Late Harvest Vidal.
905.856.3874 www.cilento.com

P.S. Fashion+Food+Drink: If you'd like to add a little food, fashion and fun to your trip, step into the huge, disco-like clothing shop called Motor Oil. Very sporty. Everyone needs a new pair of jeans. Part of the shop is a stylish, arty 'cool Italian' café called **Americani.**
688 Chrislea Road, Woodbridge 905.264.9764

wine events **calendar**

These and other events are posted on my web site: www.billysbestbottles.com (in the 'coming events/workshops' section).

JANUARY + FEBRUARY
Niagara Ice Wine Celebrations *905.688.0212 www.niagarawinefestival.com*
Guelph Wine Gala *519.821.7570*
Niagara's Days of Wine & Roses *905.468.4263*
Pacific Northwest Wine Fair *Roy Thompson Hall, Toronto 416.410.4630*

MARCH + APRIL
Ontario's Cuvée *Niagara-on-the-Lake 1.800.361.6645*
Toronto Food & Wine Show *416.229.2060 or 1.800.896.7469*
German Wine Festival *Roy Thompson Hall, Toronto 905.815.1581*
Vancouver Playhouse International Wine Fest *604.873.3311*
The Toronto Hospital Wine Classic *416.340.3935*
Burlington Wine and Food Expo *905.634.7736*

MAY
Santé: Bloor-Yorkville Wine Festival *416.928.3555 ext.24 www.santewinefestival.net*
California Wine Fair *Ottawa + Toronto 1.800.558.2675*
New Zealand Wine Fair, Toronto *705.444.5255*
Wine & Food 'Tastings' *Elmhurst Inn, Ingersoll 519.539.7469*

JUNE
Apple Blossom Fruit Wine & Food Festival *Archibald Orchards & Winery, Bowmanville 905.263.2396*
Southwestern Ontario Food & Wine Extravaganza *Bellemere Winery, London 519.473.2273*

Theatre Aquarius Vine Dining *Hamilton 905.522.7529 or 1.800.465.7529*
Toronto Taste *416.408.2594*
Theatre Beyond Words *Wine Auction Niagara-on-the-Lake 1.800.268.5774*
New Vintage Niagara Celebrations *Gala Wine Tasting and Winery Passports 905.688.0212 www.grapeandwine.com*

JULY + AUGUST

Hillebrand's Annual Jazz & Blues Festivals *Niagara 905.468.7123*
Niagara's Unforgettable Vineyard Weekends *416.777.6342 or 905.684.8070*
Festival Du Vin Des Laurentides *1.800.363.7777*
Festa Buckhorn *Buckhorn Community Centre (near Peterborough) 705.657.8455*
Festival Epicure *Windsor www.festivalepicure.com*
Slow Food Picnic *slowfoodontario@hotmail.com*
Australian Wine Experience *416.323.1155 ext. 317*

SEPTEMBER

Ontario Wine Festival *Southbrook Winery 905.832.2458*
Taste of Sault Ste. Marie *705.946.2503*
Niagara Grape & Wine Festival *St. Catharines 905.688.0212 or 416.777.634*

OCTOBER + NOVEMBER + DECEMBER

Okanagan Wine Festival *Penticton, B.C. 604.860.5999*
North Bay Wine Gala *Capital Centre 705.474.1944*
Ottawa Art Gallery Wine Auction *613.233.8699*
Thunder Bay 'Wine Affair' *807.684.4444*
Ottawa Wine & Food Show *613.567.6408*
Toronto Symphony Wine Auction & Tastings *416.593.7769*
Australian Wine Fair *Toronto 416.323.3909 ext. 303*
Vinhos De Espana *Great Hall of Hart House, U of Toronto 416.979.3353 ext. 380*
Gourmet Food + Wine Expo *Toronto 416.410.0405 www.foodandwineshow.ca*
Ports of Wine Festival *Halifax 1.800.567.5874*
Bowling for Beaujolais *(my bash) 416.530.1545 www.billysbestbottles.com*

food + wine

handy things to know

Happy Couples

A General Guide

Tips

Creating Flow

In Season

food+ wine

Pairing wine with food is challenging because there are so many weird and wonderful combinations in dishes. Even the 'experts' get baffled. There is certainly no magic formula. Your best bet is to use common sense and hope for the best – it usually works, and if not, it's because you did not think it through. In the next few pages you'll find the common sense guide that I follow, starting with the most important.

CONSIDER EVERYTHING – MOOD + WINE

The setting, the season, the nature of the event, your style, guest's expectations are some considerations that must be taken into account. The music you play might have a great influence on how the wine and food get along. In the end it is more about the desired effect or appropriateness than a scientific matching of wine with food.

ELEMENTARY MY DEAR WATSON!

The food that you select (at home or in a restaurant) is usually a reflection of your mood and needs. Pay attention to what you're 'in the mood for' and it will tell you what you need. For instance, the desire for steak suggests a need for nourishment – therefore, your wine should be nourishing too. A rich red. If pizza is what you fancy this suggests a more playful, casual mood – the wine equivalent in this case would be a lively Italian red such as Barbera or Valpolicella. In eastern culture, this approach would be called getting in touch with your centre. It's a good thing. Think about it.

happy *couples*

Here are some first steps in food and wine pairing. As you'll see, they are all linked by mood, which is why I encourage you to find the mood of each wine you drink so you can recall it to partner a food or situation.

light 'n bright food **+** light 'n bright wine
a **summer salad**, such as Nicoise, with VINHO VERDE

brisk food **+** brisk wine
pizza or colourful **antipasto** with BARBERA

bland food **+** spicy wine
egg dishes with DRY MUSCAT or GEWURZTRAMINER

sweet food **+** tangy/salty wine
BBQ'd shrimp appetizer with FINO SHERRY

charming food **+** charming wine
grilled salmon with BEAUJOLAIS or PINOT NOIR

glamour food **+** glamour wine
BBQ'd seafood with AUSSIE CHARDONNAY

oily food **+** tart wine
smoked salmon with ONTARIO DRY RIESLING

exotic food **+** exotic wine
Moroccan couscous with PINOT NOIR

soft food **+** perky wine
burgers with BACO NOIR

macho food **+** macho wine
grilled steak with CABERNET SAUVIGNON

comfort food **+** soulful wine
roast chicken with CÔTES du RHÔNE

tangy food **+** tangy wine
pasta in tomato sauce with young CHIANTI

simple 'white' food **+** savoury wine
pork or chicken with SEMILLON

food + wine

a general guide

FRESH WHITES

Soave, Pinot Grigio, Sauvignon Blanc, Pinot Blanc, Aligoté, Auxerrois, Vinho Verde, Dry Riesling (Ontario), Chenin Blanc, Gavi, Orvieto, Chardonnay (Italy)

appetizers antipasto oysters
sole snapper Thai curries

LIVELY REDS *(lightly chilled)*

Côtes du Rhône, Côtes du Luberon, Côtes du Ventoux, Beaujolais, Gamay (Ontario), Cabernet Franc (under $12, Ontario), Valpolicella, Barbera, Chianti (not Riserva), Montepulciano D'Abruzzo, Dry Rosé

cold cuts fresh cheeses quiche
bruschetta tapas roast chicken
grilled vegetables Indian curries
pasta (tomato sauce) pizza

MEDIUM WHITES

Chardonnay (under $15), Semillon, Sauvignon Blanc, Pinot Grigio, Pinot Blanc, Dry Riesling

chicken turkey pork ham veal
pasta or white meats with cream sauce
egg dishes fish seafood

MEDIUM REDS

Dry Rosé, Cru Beaujolais, Côtes du Rhône-Villages, Pinot Noir, Rioja (under $15), Aussie Shiraz (under $15), Dao, Merlot (under $15), Zinfandel (under $15), Rhône style (from California), Baco Noir, Cabernet Franc (Ontario)

burgers + ribs with ketchup/sauce sausages beans samosas chicken veal pork turkey game grilled salmon tuna swordfish lasagna moussaka mushroom risotto Tex Mex Cajun

RICH WHITES

Chardonnay (over $15) from Ontario, California, Australia, Chile, South Africa, White Burgundy, Pouilly Fumé, Sauvignon Blanc or Fumé Blanc (over $15) from California, New Zealand, Chile, Semillon (Australia), Pinot Gris (Alsace), White Rioja (over $12)

poached salmon shrimp lobster crab grouper roast pork baked ham pasta (cream sauce) white meat with cream sauce

RICH REDS

Cabernet and Merlot (over $15 from anywhere), Aussie Shiraz (over $15), Chateauneuf du Pape, Chianti Reserva, Bordeaux, Rioja Reserva, Dao, Zinfandel, Ripasso, Amarone

beef lamb game (grilled or roasted) rich braised meats

The principle is to pair wines and foods of somewhat similar personalities and/or moods – lighthearted with lighthearted, nourishing with nourishing, fancy with fancy, etc. This guide is based on wines that are generally available in our liquor stores. Each section in the front of the book also has food recommendations for specific wines.

creating *flow*

give a great dinner party

A dinner party has its flow and each drink should contribute the right energy at the right moment. Consider the following flow chart.

aperitif

Rev up with a glass of **Ontario Dry Riesling**.

Cranks up the senses + energizes.

antipasto appetizer

Get in gear with a spirited **Gamay** or **Barbera**.

Light reds are fun. They put you in the party mood. Serve lightly chilled.

seafood course

Cruise for a while with a flashy **Chardonnay**.

The party is gathering momentum and it needs a high-octane sunshine wine like Chardonnay. Something expressive and glamorous.

meat course

Rendezvous with a handsome **Chianti, Syrah, Cabernet,** or **Ripasso**.

You're now ready for the nourishing qualities of a substantial red wine.

dessert

Park and cuddle up with a sweetie, such as a **Select Late-Harvest Vidal**.

Sweetness and charm are the ingredients needed now. A nightcap of rich, sexy flavours.

drinking in season

The seasons contribute a lot to our moods and the following are a few drinking ideas that you may like to explore.

spring

In the first warm days of April or May, I like to take a bottle of **Sauvignon Blanc** out into the garden and pour myself a big glass – and I taste Spring.

With **Vinho Verde**, **Pinot Grigio** and **Dry Rosé** in my ice bucket, every summer day is perfect!

summer

fall

I greet falling leaves and falling temperatures with the red wines of the **Rhône** – such as Rasteau.

Roast chicken with Chardonnay or grilled salmon with Beaujolais, ***taste good any day*** *of the year.*

Hearty local **Baco** or Italy's **Ripasso** offer the rustic character that gladdens and warms the heart in the icy Winter months.

winter

food+ wine tips

off to a good start

The first wine you serve at dinner, at a party, or even on a picnic should be novel. A possible new experience for your guests. People are open to novelty at the beginning – they want a surprise. They know that you're going to give them something nice later. A simple way to provide novelty in the summer months is to start with a chilled lively red. Give 'em Chardonnay later.

the BBQ

Lively, fruity and cheerful wines work best with BBQ'd foods and moods. It's best if they have a sweet impression because that's a good contrast with the charred flavours. Local Cabernet Franc or Baco, Côtes du Rhône, Valpolicella Ripasso, Californian Syrah or a lighter style Aussie Shiraz are good choices with red meat. Beaujolais or Barbera are my favourite wines with white meats. Fans of white wine cannot go wrong with a rich Chardonnay or Semillon.

get your party started

With so many good, inexpensive Sparkling wines around *(see page 15)*, it's a pity that more people don't start their events with a glass of something such as Prosecco. I asked Larry Mawby (maker of Sparking wine in Northern Michigan) why people are reluctant to enjoy reasonably priced sparkling wines on a daily basis. "People are afraid that the occasion is not worthy of the wine."

Sparkling wine with food is not well understood. The yeasty, fleshy flavour in Spanish sparklers is an ideal partner for tapas or other Mediterranean appetizers. The acid and fizz in the wine make a refreshing swipe through the oil and garlic. This style of sparkler is also good with savoury, pastry appetizers of the quiche or Greek variety, and with tempura or sushi. Again, the wine cuts the fat, butter or batter.

wine for chocolate

Buy some fancy truffles, arrange them nicely on a plate and serve with a chilled glass of Framboise. Heavenly. **Southbrook Winery Framboise, Ontario** (#341024 375ml/ $15.45).

gewurzin' *about*

People are always trying to pair up Gewurztraminer with spicy foods. Forget it. Gewurztraminer is the Aires of wine – it wants all your attention. **Jackson-Triggs 2002 Gewurztraminer 'Black Label', Niagara** (#526260 Fresh White $9.95) is a wonderful summertime drink – in the daytime or early evening. Lovely, pure vibrant flavours. **Miguel Torres 2001 Gewurz-traminer, Chile** (#605584 Rich White $11.75) is luscious and charming. Definitely a bit of a trip. A lovely way to lounge. One of the great wine experiences in our stores.

my summer bucket *of refreshment*

Put four to six bottles of my 'Fresh Whites' and 'Lively Red' selections in a bucket of iced water and you have an instant, portable, summer wine bar. Let friends try all the wines by pouring just a few ounces at a time. Different moods and situations will cause certain wines to work better than others. Keep the whites and rosés well chilled, and the reds lightly chilled.

just champagne

Forget food, forget the kids, forget the world. But don't forget the Champagne! **Charles Heidsieck Brut N/V** (#31286 $47.95) is the Buick of Champagne – soft and luxurious, a smooth ride and good enough to get noticed. Great anytime.

novel & exotic experiments

Indulge in some festive, experimental or exotic wines and foods. Maybe Mexican with Zinfandel, Thai with Riesling, or Indian curry with Beaujolais.

wine *stuff*

you need to know

wine has changed

IN TASTE

Sometime in the past decade, modern-style wines took over. Wines perfumed with the vanilla and buttered toast flavour of oak have become the norm. Wine is now more glamorous, a bit sweeter, and a lot easier to like. It seems to be following the entertainment business with its focus on bigness, glitz and spectacle. This is risky. Every day in everyone's life does not need to be all bright and colourful. Wines need to echo all our moods and situations. Have Italian wine at least once a week.

IN SELECTION

New frontiers are opening up all the time so there are always new bargains. Wine got better when France lost its monopoly. She ruled the business for too long, and almost ruined it. Ironically, the places that gave us better wine (Australia and California) are now doing exactly what France did – overcharging and producing dull wines. Meanwhile, France has learned how to make good everyday wine and is now the good guy. Italy has always been a player, Portugal and Spain are trying hard, and New Zealand rocks. The growth of our local wines has been the greatest joy of all. It makes wine more real for people who have never travelled to Europe.

IN THE GUIDELINES

Are there guidelines that one can follow such as, small producers are better than large ones? Or hot climates are better than cool ones? No. Sorry. In the old days there was a nice clear distinction between the good guys and the bad guys, but these days everyone has the potential to get it right – if they try. Wine has changed and the old guidelines and beliefs are no longer reliable. For example, the big wineries are often good, the small are often bad. An unknown Sicilian wine can be better than a fancy Californian. So approach wine with a full heart and an empty head. Anything is possible.

The only thing you can be sure of is that the 'old rules' are no longer useful.

AND IN CONVENIENCE
Annually, about five percent of wines are spoiled by a fungus that grows in corks. The industry has at last addressed the problem by bottling some of its wines with screw caps. Australia and New Zealand are the leaders in this venture and are putting their 'fresh-style' wines, Riesling and Sauvignon, in screw cap bottles. It makes a lot of sense to offer wines for immediate consumption – and where freshness is important, with a sterile and convenient closure. Wolf Blass 2003 Riesling is the first of the new screw caps in our stores. Mr. Blass continues to be a leader.

if you're just **getting started** *in wine*

TRY LOTS OF DIFFERENT WINES AT FIRST using my WINE SPECTRUM chart as a guide to what to expect. Always taste at least two wines so you have a contrast. Note what works for you and try to figure out why. "I am enjoying this because . . . ." Look not only for wines to enjoy but wine and situations that excite you. A beer lover once told me that he had become interested in wine after a good experience with Gewurztraminer (two bottles) while watching hockey on T.V.
P.S. Practise my '20 Steps to Winedom', on pages 142 -144.

CHART YOUR OWN COURSE. Wine pleasure is as personal as music pleasure. Would you buy all the same CDs as your neighbour? Build your own repertoire of wine wisdom. Indulge in your own fancies and frolics. Look for wines that fit nicely into your life.

FIND A MENTOR. Learning about wine is a process of experiencing and questioning. Every bottle brings us a series of questions – that's why you need a buddy who can supply some answers. Email me if you wish: info@billysbestbottles.com

important **service details**

3 steps to success

1. QUANTITY

How many bottles should you buy for a party?
The LCBO suggests 'up to half a bottle per person.' That's a bit stingy. I cannot see a party getting off the ground on that quantity. Father Farrar Capon, an American Episcopal priest and author of many books on theology and gastronomy, decrees, "One bottle per person must always be your rule, otherwise your party will end with a whimper instead of a bang. The worst parties I have attended have invariably been those at which the host, out of ignorance or principle (one is as bad as the other), provided a mere two bottles of wine for six people."

P.S. Remember you are responsible if your guests drive home drunk.

2. GLASSWEAR

The appropriate glassware does a lot for wine.
Your enjoyment of red wine is guaranteed to increase if you invest in a few big – the bigger the better – wine goblets. Check out the Riedel line, and if that's too expensive, look for something cheaper but similar in size and feel. (*Caban* stores have fantastic $5 glasses.) You might feel self-conscious drinking from a big glass but the pleasure of the wine will quickly cure that. For white wine, I'm very happy with a tall, slender tumbler. It seems to echo the freshness of the wine. The worst glasses in the world are the dinky things that they give you at wine shows. They seem to make the wine unhappy.

3. TEMPERATURE

When colder is cooler.
Everyone knows that white wines taste best cold, but red wines also need a degree of chilling. As a

rough guide, I give nearly all my reds ten minutes in the freezer. That's right, the freezer. It's fast and won't damage the wine. Reds taste brighter, livelier and more exciting when they are slightly cool, at 'cellar temperature'. Discover this for yourself – you won't believe the difference in taste.

wine serving temperatures

20^{c}		sweet reds	**rich reds**
18^{c}			
16^{c}			**medium reds**
14^{c}	rich chardonnays		
12^{c}	medium whites		**light reds**
10^{c}		rosé	
8^{c}	light whites		
6^{c}	sparkling		**sweet whites**
4^{c}			

P.S. If you still don't believe in the need to lightly chill most reds, try this test. Pour a glass of tap water without letting it run first. Let the water run a while and fill a second glass. Now taste both. The first (which will be at room temperature) will taste flat and unappetizing. The second glass of 'cool' water will be much livelier – it will have vitality.

the good host

*a few **dos** and **donts***

A GLASS PLEASE.

Lovely home, good food, interesting company, lots of open wines but not a glass to be seen. Don't let your guests start their evening off badly. Get a clean, decent quality wineglass into your guest's hands within 10 seconds of arrival. Why not put out a tray of glasses and keep it stocked?

DON'T OVERFILL.

A full glass of wine robs the drinker of enticing fragrances and is as unappetizing as food piled too high on a plate. Wine is best enjoyed an inch at a time.

OUT OF THE DARK.

Wine, like food, is more appetizing when brightly lit. A well-lit setting makes wine and food feel more flavourful.

STINKY GLASSES.

Detergent leaves an unpleasant smell in glassware that can be difficult to get rid of. It helps if you do not stack glasses upside down and if you rotate them instead of always taking them from the front row. Best solution of all is to 'prime' your glasses with half an ounce of wine. Priming simply means coating the inside of the glass with a trace of wine. You may use the same splash of wine for your partner's glass, then chuck the wine.

DON'T PLAY IT SAFE.

I hear it all the time, "...this wine won't offend anyone." Wimpy wine does offend because it's boring, and if you're not offering excitement what kind of a host are you? We live in a golden age of wine, why not enjoy it?

GOOD PRESENTATION.

Have you ever noticed how a display of wine bottles at the entrance of a restaurant seems to excite the senses? Adopt the idea when entertaining. For dinner parties, have the aperitif wine on ice beside the glassware, ready to pour. Place dinner reds (opened, without the cork) on a sideboard to catch the eye.

GOOD PREPARATION.

Chilling wine, cleaning glassware, opening bottles, etc. takes more time than we think. Start well ahead. Water added to ice will speed up the chilling.

NOT JUST RICH.

Too much rich wine tires the senses and exhausts the body. Always include brisk wines at your events and save the 'couch wines' till near the end.

PENNY PINCHING.

Be thrifty for your everyday needs, but when entertaining your friends don't be afraid to break that ten dollar barrier. It does get noticed.

talk about it

the *traditional* way to taste

(and talk about) wine is to analyze the components and report on the findings. This is not much different from the way works of art or restaurant meals are reviewed. While this method does help establish various aspects of the experience, it seldom results in taking you to the heart of the matter.

a *better* way

to grasp the essence of something is to look at the bigger picture. Over years of tasting I've been drawn to a direct approach which consists of jumping into the middle of things. I've found that if you start on the outside you often cannot get to the heart, and this is where you want to be. Some of the best descriptions of wine have come from people who could not analyze a wine to save their lives. They simply give an honest response to an experience just as someone would give to a Rolling Stones concert. Or, as Matisse said, they 'observed . . . and felt the innermost nature of the experience.' Many people have difficulty doing this with wine because they believe there is a proper wine language and a correct response to each wine. They fear giving the wrong answer.

If a wine feels happy, comforting or dreary, go ahead and say so. There are more meaningful expressions than what the experts come up with. And your friends will know what you mean.

"I do not want to deconstruct the pleasure of wine by trying to work out whether the aromas smell of bananas or apricots. If you analyze too much, you end up destroying the pleasure...." Lionel Poilane (famous French baker)

think about it

only *one* wine!

When people tell me they have a favourite wine and it's the only one they buy, I'm astounded. To drink only one wine is like listening to only one song – over and over. Wine, like music, is made in a huge variety of styles to suit every mood and occasion. Develop a repertoire and you'll have way more fun.

your favourite *is not always* the best choice

Different occasions call for different wines. It's not OK to serve your favourite wine on every occasion. Shiraz gets poured a lot because it's comforting. But not all situations need comfort – there are other moods. And therefore other wine needs. When you learn to match wine to mood, you will have lots of favourites.

stocking a cellar *full of fancy wine* can be an interesting hobby, but!

If you talk to anyone who's done it they will usually admit that they seldom find occasions to drink the special wines they have collected. It never seems to be appropriate. A better practice is to invest in good wine for your daily needs. Drink something you really like more often. Live for today.

Billy's 20 steps to winedom

Consider this a summary of my book. Everything you need to know in a few pages.

1. How does it feel?

The communion between wine and people is feelings. Put aside the conventional belief that wine's statement is flavour – the essence or character of a wine can only be felt. It's the feeling of a wine that connects it to our moods and events.

2. Exercise daily.

Make wine a daily companion. With so much wine to enjoy you'll never make a dent in it unless you drink it everyday.

3. Think about your experience of the wine, not the wine itself.

Different kinds of music create different emotional responses – this is also true of wine. Dry Riesling is a lift, Shiraz is soothing, Sauvignon challenges, etc.

4. The two-step.

Most situations call for the wine two-step – refreshing wine to begin, and nourshing wine later.

5. Meet it halfway.

Wine like music, is interactive. It's not something that once purchased you can say, 'Now I've got it'. You have nothing until you put the wine into context with the mood and the company – and with thought. It's what YOU bring to the wine that will make it shine or not, and give it value. The $10 bottle can deliver a hundred dollars worth of pleasure, and vice versa. Forget expertise and work on your playing skills. Aspire to become your own wine DJ.

6. Enjoy wine freely.

Get some experience and try lots of different wines at first. But avoid mental stress – you do not need to know wine to enjoy it. Knowing can come later.

7. Explore beyond the nice n' smooth.

Go beyond the top 40 hits. While easy wines provide comfort, the challenging ones keep us stimulated. Emotion and tension are as important in wine as in music. That's why God gave us Italy.

8. Avoid prestige wine.

And the mob that follow it. Wine attracts a lot of snobs, geeks and people with too much money. The mind of the snob drinker tells him to like the snob wine. While the mind of the novice is free to support the good feeling of an everyday wine.

9. Make a match.

Great times do not need great wine – just the one that works for the mood and moment. Matching wine and moment is what creates good times, not the price of the bottle.

10. Learn by contrast.

Have several wines on the go so you can experience contrasting styles. And discover how there is always one wine that's better for the moment than the rest. Opened, refrigerated wines keep well for 3 to 4 days.

11. Get off to a good start.

The first wine that you serve at a dinner or party should be novel – a possible new experience for your guests. People are open to novelty at the beginning – they want a surprise. They know that you are going to give them something nice and more familiar later.

12. Be playful.

Drinking should be one of our most playful times, so let playful wines be your main purchase.

13. Match wine with food and mood.

If you are drinking the wine that's right for your mood, it will also be right for the food. Because you will have made a good food choice based on your mood. Got that?

14. Keep your talk plain.

Many people have difficulty expressing their feelings about a wine because they believe there is a correct response to each wine. They fear giving the wrong answer. If a wine feels happy, comforting, or dreary, go ahead and say so. These are more meaningful expressions than what the experts come up with – and better than "like it or hate it". And your friends will know what you mean.

15. The two wine camps.

Wine can be divided into two camps – the old world wines and the new world wines. Old world wines (France, Italy, etc.) are very dry and are often challenging. But like European movies they can be thought provoking. New world wines (California, Australia, etc.) are easier to like and they taste a lot sweeter. These are crafted to appeal to a culture that drinks a lot of fruit juice and pop. New world wines work well with a lot of today's spicy/hot foods while old world wines are happiest with traditional roasts and grills.

16. In case of emergency . . .

Grab the Beaujolais. Get a baguette (and maybe some Brie). Leave your worries on the doorstep. Direct your picnic to the sunny side of the street.

17. Be open minded, take chances.

Seek out new experiences, something you've not experienced before. Wine is about change – it helps us change. It's a great outlet for imagination. And of course for relaxation, contemplation, communion and enchantment.

18. Celebrate the everyday.

In wine and in life. Wine's origins are in peasant culture – an old wooden table, the shade of a tree and good company. Wine is about sociability and celebrating the everyday.

19. There is no best wine.

Only wines that are best for the moment.

20. It's the trip that counts.

Chart your own course. Enjoy the good and keep learning from what you don't like. Tomorrow you will have different tastes. It will always be a bit confusing, a bit challenging – just like life. Which is part of the excitement. Enjoy it.

last call *final words*

The love of chocolate, the love of wine, the lover!

Many of the most popular wines out there today taste a lot like chocolate. Aussie Shiraz certainly does. I don't want this flavour in my red wine any more than I would welcome chocolate sauce on my chicken or burger. But I'd wager that Aussie wine would not be half as popular if it were not for the chocolate flavour. I recently read an interview with a movie star who said that he liked 'rich, weighty wines that taste like chocolate in a bottle.' The same guy also said that he 'likes wines that make love to my palate.' At first I thought that was quite poetic but later I realized that what he'd said was he's into wine orgasm more than wine lovemaking. I better explain.

The rich, soft, creamy, chocolate-style wines can drive your mouth crazy with delight but they seldom go beyond that single sensation. Just as a good lover will bring more than niceness to a date, a good wine should do more than make love to the tongue. The intellect and imagination should also be excited. Conversation and foreplay must be part of the experience – maybe even a little roughness or toughness. Certainly some play and humour. All will not be delivered in the first glass, let alone the first sip. There will be a tease, and an unfolding. There will be several acts.

The popular Shiraz/Merlot/Cabernet wines of today offer the quick bang. There's enjoyment for sure but be aware – it's not lovemaking. That's something you have to seek out in wines that are more than just nice tongueteasers.

WARNING

The wine business moves so fast that anything you think you know is already no longer valid. The new stuff keeps streaming down. More than half of what you've read in this handbook is sure to be invalid by the end of 2004.

PLEASE DESTROY

this book at end of 2004 and get the new edition. It will do us both good.

USE THE $5 DISCOUNT COUPON

on the back of this page when ordering the new 2005 edition from me.

(Expires November 30, 2004)

For information about Billy's Best Bottles wineletter, upcoming events and current projects, please visit

www.billysbestbottles.com

or contact me at

BILLY'S BEST BOTTLES

589 Markham Street

Toronto ON

M6G 2V9

P 416 530 1545

F 416 530 1575

E info@billysbestbottles.com

Find price and vintage updates of the wines recommended in this book in the handbook section of www.billysbestbottles.com.

If you enjoyed this book

please buy a copy for a friend.

NEXT YEAR'S BOOK

SAVE 5 BUCKS!

Use this coupon when you order next year's edition.

We'll be shipping the new books in early December. Buy 10 for your friends and save lots! Visit **www.billysbestbottles.com** for order forms and details – or give us a call at 416.530.1545 to have a order form sent to you.

Valid for book ordered from ***Billy's Best Bottles*** *before December 1st, 2004. One coupon per order per customer.*
Sorry, no cash value.

Sláinte!

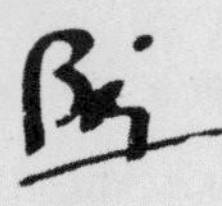

Come back!

Billy's Best Bottles
589 Markham Street Toronto Ontario M6G 2L7

P 416 530 1545
F 415 530 1575
E info@billysbestbottles.com

www.billysbestbottles.com

index

wines by category

fresh whites *pages 13 - 29*

lively reds *pages 31- 41*

lively reds continued

> Spinelli 2001 Montepulciano D'Abruzzo 'Quartana', Italy
> Thorin 2002 Côtes du Ventoux 'Grand Reserve De Challieres, France
> Torres 2002 Rosado 'De Casta', Spain
> Xanadu 2002 Rosé of Cabernet, Western Australia

medium whites *pages 43 - 59*

> Bodegas Etchart 2002 Torrontés, Argentina
> Bouchard Père & Fils 2002 Macon Lugny St. Pierre, France
> Calvet Reserve 2002 Bordeaux, France
> Cave Spring 2002 Riesling Reserve, Niagara
> Ch. Grand Renom 2001 Sauvignon, Bordeaux, France
> Colio 'Harrow Estates' 2002 Chardonnay, Ontario
> Dom. Boyar 2002 Chardonnay, Bulgaria
> Dom. Paul Mas 'La Forge' 2002 Chardonnay, France
> Dunavar 2002 Pinot Blanc, Hungary
> Fortant de France 2002 Chardonnay, France
> Georges Duboeuf 2001 Côtes du Rhône, France
> Georges Duboeuf 2002 Macon-Villages, France
> Hardys 2002 Chardonnay/Semillon 'Stamp Series', Australia
> Henry of Pelham 2002 Chardonnay 'Non Oaked', Niagara
> Henry of Pelham 2002 Riesling Reserve, Niagara
> Hillebrand 2002 Riesling 'Trius', Niagara
> Jackson-Triggs 2002 Chardonnay 'Black Label', Niagara
> JeanJean 2002 Chardonnay 'Arabesque', France
> Marques de Riscal 2002 Rueda, Spain
> Mission Hill 2002 Sauvignon Blanc, Okanagan Valley,
> Nederburg 2002 Sauvignon Blanc, South Africa
> Pelee Island 2002 Chardonnay 'Premium Select', Ontario
> Peter Lehmann 2001 Semillon, Barossa, Australia
> Rothschild 2002 Chardonnay, France
> Santa Rita 2003 Sauvignon Blanc Reserva, Chile
> Santi 2002 Pinot Grigio 'Sortesele', Italy
> Serego Alighieri 2002 Bianco, Italy
> Talus 2002 Pinot Grigio, California
> Tyrrell's 2002 Long Flat White, Australia
> Vallagarina 2002 Pinot Grigio 'Nuvole', Italy
> Villa Maria 2002 Sauvignon Blanc, New Zealand
> Xanadu 'Secession' 2001 Semillon/Chardonnay, Western Australia

medium reds *pages 61 - 75*

> Agricole Vallone 2000 Salice Salentino 'Vereto', Italy
> Aveleda 2000 Douro 'Charamba', Portugal
> Bodegas Piqueras 2000 Castillo Almansa Reserva, Spain
> Brusco Dei Barbi 2000 Tuscany, Italy
> Cantina Tollo 2000 Montepulciano D'Abruzzo 'Colle Secco', Italy
> Chateau Canada 2000 Bordeaux, France
> Ch. Des Charmes 2001 Cabernet/Merlot, Niagara
> Duca Di Castelmonte 2000 Cent'are, Italy
> Fetzer 2001 Pinot Noir 'Valley Oaks', California
> Hardys 2001 'Nottage Hill' Shiraz, Australia
> Henry of Pelham 2002 Baco Noir, Niagara
> Henry of Pelham 2002 Cabernet/Merlot 'Meritage, Niagara
> KWV 2001 Roodeberg, South Africa
> M. Chapoutier 2000 'Rasteau' Côtes du Rhône-Villages, France
> Osborne 2000 'Solaz' Tempranillo/Cabernet, Spain
> Pasqua 2001 Primitivo 'Terre Del Sole' Salentino, Italy
> Pelee Island 2002 Merlot, Ontario
> Pillitteri 2001 Cabernet/Merlot, Niagara
> Rocca Delle Macie 2001 Chianti Classico,Italy
> Rosemount 2002 Shiraz/Cabernet, Australia
> Sogrape 2000 Dao 'Duque De Viseu', Portugal
> Sogrape 2000 Douro 'Mateus Signature', Portugal
> Sogrape 2000 Douro 'Vila Regia', Portugal
> Talus 2002 Shiraz, California
> Torres 2001 Sangre de Toro, Spain
> Umani Ronchi 2001 Rosso Conero 'Serrano', Italy

rich whites *pages 77 - 83*

> Black Opal 2002 Chardonnay, Australia
> Henry of Pelham 2002 Chardonnay 'Barrel Fermented', Niagara
> Louis Jadot 2000 Bourgogne Chardonnay, France
> Santa Rita 2002 Chardonnay 'Reserva', Chile
> Santa Rita 2003 Chardonnay '120', Chile
> Sebastiani 2000 Chardonnay Sonoma, California
> Simonsig 2001 Chardonnay, South Africa
> Wolf Blass 2002 Chardonnay, Australia
> Wynns Connawarra 2001 Chardonnay, Australia

rich reds *pages 85 - 97*

> Bertani 2000 Valpolicella Secco, Italy
> Cesari 2000 'Mara' Ripasso Valpolicella, Italy
> Ch. De Gougauzaud 2002 Minervois, France
> Cline 2000 Syrah, California
> Cline 2001 Zinfandel, California
> Concha Y Toro 2002 Merlot 'Casillero Del Diablo', Chile

rich reds continued

> E. Guigal 2000 Côtes du Rhône, France
> Familia Rutini 2002 Merlot 'Trumpeter', Argentina
> Frescobaldi 2001 Rosso Di Montalcino 'Campo Ai Sassi', Italy
> Grant Burge 2001 Merlot, Australia
> Hardys 'Crest' 2000 Cabernet/Shiraz/Merlot, Australia
> Houghton 2001 Shiraz, Australia
> Pasqua 2000 'Sagramoso' Ripasso, Italy
> R.H. Philips 2000 Syrah, California
> Ravenswood 2001 Zinfandel, California
> Roberta Skalli 2001 Merlot, France
> Santa Rita 2001 Cabernet Sauvignon Reserve, Chile
> Serego Alighieri 200 Valpolicella Classico, Italy
> Vinas Del Vero 2000 Cabernet Sauvignon 'Somontano', Spain
> Wynns 2000 Cabernet Sauvignon, Australia

fringe wines *pages 99 - 107*

> Bodegas Jacques & François Lurton 2002 Pinot Gris, France
> Cave Spring 2000 Select Late Harvest Riesling 'Indian Summer', Niagara
> Cave Spring 2001 Off-Dry Riesling, Niagara
> Colio Estates 2001 Late Harvest Vidal, Ontario
> Deleforce Rich Tawny, Portugal
> Fonseca Bin 27 Port, Portugal
> Gonzalez Byass Fino 'Tio Pepe', Spain
> Graham's 10-Year-Old Tawny, Portugal
> Henry of Pelham 2000 Special Select Late Harvest Vidal', Niagara
> Martini & Rossi's Demi-Sec, Italy
> Pelee Island 2002 Gewurztraminer, Ontario
> Sogrape 'Mateus Rosé', Portugal
> Southbrook Winery Framboise, Ontario
> Taylor Fladgate 1997 Late Bottle Vintage, Portugal
> William & Humber 'Dry Sack', Spain

index

wines by country

CANADA: ONTARIO

CANADA: BRITISH COLUMBIA

ARGENTINA

AUSTRALIA

SPAIN

USA